25.95

The Business of Running a Library

The Business of Running a Library

A Handbook for Public Library Directors

by

Paul John Cirino

McFarland & Company, Inc., Publishers
Jefferson, North Carolina, and London

British Library Cataloguing-in-Publication data are available

Library of Congress Cataloguing-in-Publication Data

Cirino, Paul John, 1938–
  The business of running a library : a handbook for public library
directors / Paul John Cirino.
      p.   cm.
  Includes index.
  ISBN 0-89950-648-8 (lib. bdg. : 55# alk. paper) ∞
  1. Public libraries—Administration—Handbooks, manuals, etc.
I. Title.
Z678.C57   1991
027.4—dc20   91-52768
                                                              CIP

Manufactured in the United States of America

McFarland & Company, Inc., Publishers
  Box 611, Jefferson, North Carolina 28640

This book is dedicated to my Mom and Dad, who gave me values and taught me how to care about other people,

and to Dick, Myron, and Bob, and those like them, who always fought the good fight against tough odds to give their communities great public libraries,

and to Mickey and Sandy, and all of our initial crew, who were always there when I needed them,

and, most especially, to my pal Nora, without whose valued advice and encouragement, this probably would never have been completed,

and to all the gang at the Middle Country Public Library, who have proven that this stuff really works,

and, lastly, to my wonderful wife, Lynne, and our children, P. J., Chris and Jennifer, who had to listen to me talk about this for oooh, so long!

Table of Contents

1. Bureaucracy versus Leadership

*"Bureaucracy is the art of making
the possible impossible"*
—Anonymous

This is not a textbook. It is a survival handbook for public library directors. There has been little written about the the real world experience of managing the modern American public library. There are, of course, works on this subject, but all too often, they have been written by intellectuals who have had little or no contact with the actual consumers of public library services, much less real world experience in creating and administering such services.

The present sad state of many of our public libraries is the result of the failure of the people operating the libraries to know what they are actually supposed to be doing. This is not an uncommon failure in private business, as well as the public sector. Management consultant Peter Drucker has been asking managers to answer these same simple questions for over thirty years:

What business is the company in?
What does the customer pay the company to do?
What is the value to the customer of the company's
   products or services?

What may seem to be obvious, basic, common sense questions that should be clearly articulated at the outset, are, in fact, often overlooked.

Some professional librarians will be shocked by the comparisons that are here being made between public libraries and private businesses. Public libraries are, after all, not private businesses, but public institutions, and of course, have loftier goals than merely the pursuit of profits. What these loftier goals are supposed to be varies greatly from institution to institution, and are in most cases, poorly articulated and largely incorrect, and thus are detrimental to quality public library service rather than serving to enhance it.

The public library is one of the few public service agencies that can function much like a private sector organization. Public libraries do not have captive audiences, only captive taxpayers. They must attract patrons, or to use a more appropriate term, customers. A library is a unique public service, because use of its services is on an entirely voluntary basis. If public libraries have developed the proper mechanisms to respond effectively to consumer demand, then their services will be more heavily utilized. Libraries must develop service programs that their customers find useful. Some libraries are successful in responding to consumer demand and some aren't. That is the main reason for the great variations from library to library in utilization statistics.

There is only one very important difference between libraries and private businesses that should be noted. Private businesses that hold monopoly power can fail to display technological or allocative efficiency and still stay in business, as a result of their total control of the market. Private companies that must compete in the marketplace must do so efficiently or they will lose their customers and their profits to competing companies that are more efficient. Libraries, on the other hand, are government monopolies. As with most monopolies, efficiency of operation usually rates only fair to poor, and risk taking, innovation and creativity are not common commodities. These are all hallmarks of well run businesses.

Most of the library professionals are content to sit back and become the quintessential bureaucrats that government monopolies seem to breed so efficiently. All too many of our public libraries operate like the government monopolies they are: inefficient, bloated bureaucracies, where innovation and change are avoided rather than revered. Libraries, like other areas of government, are inherently inefficient because of the absence of incentive for profit and the lack of competition.

Government has a captive audience. If your house is on fire you don't shop around for the best fire department. You utilize the one assigned to your area. When you go to the motor vehicle department to renew your driver's license or car registration, you don't choose the one where the staff treats you with the most courtesy or processes your application the most rapidly and efficiently. You have no choice, and the attitude of the staff at these institutions usually reflects the fact that they know they have this monopoly power. Power, in the hands of petty bureaucrats, is indeed repugnant, but we are forced to endure it time and time again.

Anyone who has to deal with the welfare department, the social security department, or any number of other governmental departments, supposedly there to serve the public, can attest to the usual rudeness and indifference of the staff. It has become the rule rather than the exception. It is this essential difference in the administration of a public library, if recognized and capitalized upon, that will allow public libraries to rise far above other governmental agencies in their ability to effectively respond to consumer demand and to offer high quality, efficiently delivered services.

It is this failure to recognize the obvious, the failure to recognize the essential difference between public libraries and other government agencies that contributes to the introduction of what we might call the "B" (for Bureaucrat) Factor: how seemingly intelligent and well meaning people can behave quite foolishly when it comes to the administration of their enterprises. They not only do not understand what they are supposed to be doing, but how they can do it in the most cost effective manner. Librarians who sometimes do ask these questions often come to the wrong conclusions because they have allowed their intellectual prejudices and preconceived notions to mask simple, obvious answers.

The wise have pontificated for centuries over the idea that there is nothing so uncommon as common sense. If you really know where you are supposed to be headed, and what you need to do to reach that destination, you have a much better chance of getting there. Once librarians become impressed with their educational credentials and obsessed with altruistic goals on the mission of the public library, the "B" Factor will all too often take over and guide them down the wrong path.

What this book is about is leadership. If you want to be a successful manager in a bureaucracy, then forget about leadership. Do those things that will be necessary to make you a successful bureaucrat, not a successful leader. Allow the "B" Factor to take over and your main efforts will be directed towards protecting yourself and your bureaucracy, rather than efficiently satisfying the needs of your customers.

The "B" Factor is not unique to public institutions. It pervades the business world as well, usually being more prevalent in larger corporations. It is one of main reasons that the United States is losing to the Japanese and other foreign competitors in the world trade markets.

Mark Green, in a December 3, 1986, article in the *New York Times*, outlined the situation quite clearly.

> Takeovers . . . are clearly symptoms of a more serious disease afflicting American business—a rash of elephantine, inefficient, and self-serving corporate bureaucracy. Since the public now interprets the word bureaucracy to stand specifically for "federal bureaucracy," we thought it necessary to coin a different word, "corpocracy," to describe Washington's corporate cousin—those companies that have excessive layers of staff between managers and markets.
>
> Corpocracies have some or all of the following 10 tell-tale traits that make them easy to distinguish from trimmer firms. They are insensitive to employees; they encourage office politics, instead of productivity; they foster secrecy that stifles communication; they produce paralyzing amounts of paperwork; they diffuse responsibility through endless meetings; they neglect potential markets; they encourage short-term thinking; they shun employees who rock the boat; they isolate management from workers; and they discourage innovation. The organization of a typical corpocracy defies common sense . . . corpocracies typically conduct themselves in an economically irrational manner that retards the country's economic growth. Thus, American productivity continues to slow and the market share of our industries are declining worldwide.
>
> Top management must bear responsibility for the costs and consequences of corpocratic management. Certainly all too many managers of America's biggest corporations act on the belief that bigger is better and that there is safety in numbers. One indicator of American management's culpability: the lengthening list of Japanese companies that established plants or businesses here, operating them with American workers, as successfully as if they were in Japan.

The "B" Factor has caused America's productivity to falter. The means of production of our goods and services are all too often controlled by bureaucrats, rather than by leaders. Often these bureaucrats have very important sounding titles and impressive graduate degrees. This is an important thing to note at this point, because one surefire way to recognize those bureaucrats or corpocrats affected by the "B" Factor is that they tend to substantially derive their status from those titles, degrees, and the perks of their high offices, rather than relying on their leadership skills and productivity as a true measure of their success and importance.

The motivating factors behind my ideas concerning the administration of a public library are derived mainly from years of study in the fields of economics and labor relations, as well as a lifetime of experience as a leader. These are some of the areas that library directors should be interested in if they are to sharpen their skills. For a public library director, a master's degree in library science is of limited value in training for the responsibilities required for that position.

When I say that I have had a lifetime of experience as a leader, I actually mean just that. I learned many of the leadership skills that I use today while I was still a boy, although I did not realize it at the time. For example, when I played for a team in the town baseball league at age eleven, I was unhappy with the team's manager, also another eleven year old. When I found that others were also unhappy with his leadership, I was able to wrest control of the team from him. We won the league championship the next year and I managed summer league teams until my mid-twenties, when marriage and a knee injury forced my early retirement.

If you wanted to play sports in those days, you either organized street games or played for a team that was usually organized and managed by one of the players. This was obviously before the advent of today's more formalized leagues, which took away actual control of the teams from the children and placed it in the hands of the parents, thus depriving many children of invaluable leadership experiences.

It was through street games and other experiences like this that I unwittingly learned the skills of leadership. It was a marvelous training ground, indeed. Leadership roles were obtained by those who earned them. If little Johnny was unhappy because he felt that he should be playing third base instead of Jimmy, I had to deal with that. Not being an especially good street fighter, I had to learn to handle such disputes with tact and diplomacy. Leaders led and followers followed, not because of some title bestowed upon them, or because of an organizational structure imposed upon them by a higher authority. Leaders rose to the top because of the natural human interplay between the dominant and the submissive that was allowed to freely operate.

We learned how to follow, how to lead, how to direct the combined efforts of a group towards the successful completion of a goal: winning the game. Those who couldn't lead either learned or failed. If the leader was ineffective, there was wasted effort, lack of team spirit, dissatisfaction and low morale; usually the result was a losing record.

There were some teams, however, that although poorly managed, were still able to produce winning records. Some teams simply had such an abundance of talented players that they were able to overcome managerial insufficiencies and still win. This is also true of the public sector and the business world. Monopolies can often produce excellent services. They just can't do it efficiently. Almost anything can be made to work if the operator is given an unlimited amount of resources. Major companies may be horribly managed, yet still make a profit, for a variety of reasons.

These reasons, though many, can be boiled down to just a few basics. A company may have monopoly or oligopoly power over the markets, allowing them to sustain losses and eventually pass their costs along to the consumer, no matter how outrageous. A major U.S. computer company lost a huge portion of its market share in the early 1980s to small, innovative competitors. It was able to regain its market share even though it had not been particularly innovative or creative. It had tremendous resources that it threw into a catch-up program which succeeded. The company had high product identification and customer loyalty, so when they finally got back on track, customers flocked to them. They were able to succeed because of their huge resources. They were big and they were trusted, so they were able to recoup. Mistakes like this, which might have caused smaller companies to fail, only caused a small ripple in this company's huge profits. This can't always be accomplished, as can be shown by the recent track record of U.S. auto manufacturers.

No students of leadership or human resources management could help but cringe at the methods used by George Steinbrenner in his administration of the Yankees. Short term goals and negative motivation have been his hallmarks. He was able to win, in the short run, using these methods. He obviously fancies himself to be something of an entrepreneur. His entrepreneurial behavior and his willingness to spend huge sums of money to purchase the talent he needed to win, provided him with a team of such enormous talent that it was able to turn in winning records for a short period of time, despite a lack of real leadership. Mr. Steinbrenner, unfortunately, appears to be either unwilling or unable to effectively delegate to his staff and to positively motivate and inspire his players. His short term approach to winning, was just exactly that, a short term approach. He was able to win in the short run. In the long run, however, his lack of positive leadership has provided quite a different picture.

He cannot buy a winner every year. He must build team spirit through positive support from within, not with threats and intimidation. He must delegate responsibilities along with the authority to carry them out. He must support the decisions of his managers and staff. The hiring of nineteen managers in eighteen years does not exactly place the Yankees in the category of an organization that believes in the long term approach to leadership.

Respect and loyalty are something that a leader must earn. They cannot be forcibly extracted. They can only be given freely. The real power in an organization must come from the bottom up. Without pride in the long term accomplishments of the Yankee organization, the short term results were quickly lost, and the Yankees have not been at the top of the heap for some time. This, unfortunately, is likely to continue, unless Mr. Steinbrenner has such an unlimited pocketbook that he could buy any players he wanted. He apparently doesn't, so the Yankees are mired in discontent, being mere shadows of the great Yankee teams of yesteryear.

This also should be of prime concern in the operation of a public library. As a library director, you are in the public library business and, as such, you must be primarily concerned with the efficient operation of this business in the long run, not just the short run. Unfortunately, library directors, like many of their private sector counterparts, find little advantage in the achievement of other than short term goals. Private sector managers too often have their fates tied to their company's last quarter's profits. The short term bottom line is overemphasized at the expense of long term growth and productivity. Long term loyalty to a particular company often is of little benefit. The name of the game is look good for a few years, then move to a higher position in another company. Library directors are often faced with the same dilemma. The library director who spends the majority of his or her career working at one institution with a cooperative and helpful board of trustees is rapidly becoming a thing of the past. Schools, also, run into this same problem. The average tenure for a superintendent of schools is less than four years. It's longer for library directors, but the trend is definitely towards a shorter, not a longer tenure. This situation obviously is not conducive to the breeding of leaders who see the value of long term results. The name of the game is: show short term improvements, add a lot of credits to the resume, and move another rung up the ladder in another community.

Those cooperative, friendly boards of yesteryear have, in large part, been replaced by upwardly mobile politicians; persons elected or appointed due to special interests, or those interested in power, whose hidden agenda has more to do with ego gratification than the welfare of the library. The boards of trustees of yesteryear were largely composed of successful professionals and business people. They served on these boards, not only because they wanted to give something back to the communities that supported them, but because they realized that quality libraries, like other local services, were the foundation of real value and equity in the community. Short term savings in these areas would most surely show up later as reduced property values, and decay of the business district, to say nothing of the more serious long term effects of reducing the educational qualifications of our citizens; those qualifications being one of the most important foundations of our nations's long term growth and productivity. America has been a rich and productive country, in no small part, because we have made huge investments in human capital.

The lack of qualifications of library and school board members has become so critical that a training program through the University of Santa Clara (California) has been commissioned to train school board members in the business skills they lack. Consider the qualifications that you might look for if you were appointing someone to sit on the board of a Fortune 500 company. The person you would be looking for would have to have extensive business experience, and a clearly demonstrated record of achievement. He or she must also possess good business savvy; street smarts, if you like. Preferably, that person would also show some foresight, having a keen eye for long term goals and the future health of the company.

Such leadership skills will also stand library board members in good stead. More often than not, these skills are sorely lacking in today's board member. That is one of the reasons why, in 1985, Lee Mahon of the University of Santa Clara launched a program to provide leadership and corporate style training to school board members. It's a start in the right direction for schools and something comparable should be begun for libraries.

This book will hold a different value and be subjected to wide degrees of interpretation by the various library administrators who read it. That is because each person will find him or herself in a different type of library organization. The various sizes and organizational structures of the libraries that people happen to be working in will allow librarians to utilize either few or many of the lessons outlined here. How well they are able to function as leaders, instead of bureaucrats, will depend on their intestinal fortitude and the size of the bureaucracy that they are trying to change. Real bureaucrats can survive in almost any political climate. The more corrupt, the more tightly structured and the more political the library, the better the chances of survival for the true bureaucrat. Leaders, on the other hand, are at risk in unfavorable political climates.

If you operate a big city library, where the library board members are appointees of the mayor or the city fathers, you might find your job little more than that of a politician, maneuvering among the myriad of department heads for your share of the tax pie. Your ability to stay afloat and navigate the political waters will be the key determinant in your success or failure. There is a small likelihood that your work will be judged and rewarded based on your ability to deliver a valuable service efficiently. You wouldn't be the first leader who fell into disfavor for failing to allow the mayor to stock the library with political patronage appointees.

Those of you who are in small or medium sized libraries may find it no better. Small town library trustees, too, can be on the library board for a variety of reasons which have nothing to do with their competence. Some serve for nothing more than ego gratification. For others, library board membership can be viewed as a political stepping stone. Others may sincerely want to serve their community. There is, however, all too often a large gap between sincere intentions and the ability to carry them out.

Not all library trustees are bad. It should be understood, however, that membership on a library board has nothing to do with the individual's competence or the sincerity of his or her intentions to serve. There many trustees that are dedicated and competent. But there are also many that aren't. These are the most reprehensible, because often their hypocritical view of themselves doesn't allow them to admit that they really are politicians. The position of library trustee, whether elected or appointed, is that of a politician, although there are library trustees who practically equate their positions with those of religious figures. Loving books and libraries is no more a guarantee of success for a trustee than it is for a library director. Such attitudes allow the "B" Factor to take over and attract people to the library field that have no business being there.

A true leader will oppose bureaucrats who are straitjacketed by the committee mentality. Such a leader is taking a risk and may lose, but if a win occurs instead, what wonderful things can be accomplished. A leader not affected by the "B" Factor can change the political climate and educate trustees and staff as to the real mission of the public library: to provide services and materials that will serve to entertain and enlighten the members of the community. A library must learn to respond to the needs of the community without the constraints of a cumbersome bureaucracy. This requires courageous risk taking. Failure can result in the library director's having to find another library to direct or another profession.

Here is a true example of a success story, where courage, innovation, and fortitude paid off. A young high school history teacher worked for a public library on a part-time basis. As a result of his experiences, he was motivated to obtain a library science degree and enter the profession full-time. The library director was a leader and thus was instrumental in not only motivating and inspiring this fledgling librarian, but in helping him obtain his first full-time reference job at a neighboring library. After several years, he had the opportunity to become director of a newly created public library. He asked his mentor if there was any advice that he could give to him before he went to interview for the job. The advice was that he should insist on being nothing less than the library's CEO (chief executive officer), with much the same authority as one would find in a similar private sector position. He was not to be a figurehead administrator. His job was to run the library. He would hire and fire without political interference. There would be no political patronage appointees. The board was not to be involved in the day to day operation of the library, but rather was to formulate policy; that policy was to be formulated only after consultation with and heavy reliance on the recommendations of the director, who also should serve as the board's chief professional advisor.

As long as the division of responsibilities was clear, he would have the opportunity to be an effective leader and operate his library as efficiently as possible, free from politics. His library would grow, prosper and become a respected institution of lasting value to the community. He was told that if those terms were not acceptable to the trustees, in two years he would be no more than a political "yes" man, and would be very sorry that he took the job. Fortunately, the climate was right, so courage and good sense prevailed. Today, this gentleman is the director of a well managed and well respected library.

Everything was not always roses. He had to survive several challenges to his authority, including one call for his dismissal from trustees who resented his leadership and the increased control it entailed. You must be willing to risk the same. This director has interviewed for several higher level positions since he took this job. He was surprised to learn that his reputation and ability to exercise strong leadership was actually frowned upon by some trustees. It seemed to frighten trustees who realized that they would have to relinquish control of the library's day to day operations, a power they should not have been accorded anyway. Strong leadership is often not understood or appreciated. Unfortunately, all too many of our library politicians prefer bureaucratic "yes" men and women to be their library directors. They would rather sacrifice creativity, innovation and efficiency, than relinquish some of their political power.

Leaders actually are very frightening to politicians and bureaucrats. I have interviewed for positions where the trustees actually seemed shocked that I would have the audacity to expect that I be allowed to administer the library free from political interference. This is to some extent the result of their community activities. The route to the library board is usually found through membership in a variety of community organizations: clubs, PTAs, civic associations, and so on. Most of these organizations operate with a committee consensus of volunteers. These people are not accustomed to having paid staff, much less an executive director who is responsible for the actual day to day operation of the organization. The result, all too often, is that these people expect to involve themselves in the day to day operation of the library. Some of the more involved want to be consulted on even the most minor decisions. It is not uncommon to hear library board members discussing what kind of typewriters should be purchased or from what vendor the library should purchase its paper products. These are hardly what could be called major policy decisions.

Now that you have a general idea of some of the problems library leaders are going to face, let's take a look at them more specifically: The first is "deciding on what business you are actually in."

2. What Is the Business of a Public Library?

*"We cannot become what we need to
be by remaining what we are"*
—Max Depree

The basic problem with most public library directors is that they
do not really have a good idea of what they are supposed to be accomplishing; i.e., what are the goals of the public library? Much has
been written about the expanded role of the modern public library as
a community center, greatly expanding its stereotypical role as merely
a place to engage in some quiet research, or where one can pick up a
best seller, usually after a long wait. The parameters of that expanded
role, however, are too often determined by the librarian-bureaucrats,
rather than by the consumers of their services.

The mission of a public library is simple and clear. If librarians
follow the goals that have been identified when making leadership decisions, they will have a much better chance of providing services to their
customers that more clearly reflect their wants and needs.

*The mission of a public library is to offer materials and ser-
vices that provide for the enlightenment and entertainment of
the library's potential customers, as rapidly and efficiently as
possible.*

Libraries become sidetracked because they often fail to keep sight
of all the requirements necessary to fulfill this mission. In the public
sector, agencies are supposed to be able to provide a service of high
quality at a low cost. Many public agencies aren't even able to provide
adequate, much less superior services, and most can't provide them
efficiently. Most libraries aren't able to provide a wide array of high
quality services. Those that are able to provide quality services, for the
most part, don't provide them efficiently.

Some librarians don't like talking about the library as a business, one that must respond to the needs of its customers and do so efficiently. Libraries are a sacred cow; to some, almost akin to motherhood. Like many public services, the main goal is to provide quality services. Few are motivated to do so efficiently. Bureaucrats are usually rewarded on the basis of the size of the bureaucracy that they administer. The incentive is actually to be inefficient. If the bureaucratis able to do the job while spending less, the job will probably will be judged to be worth less, because he or she has a smaller bureaucracy. Budget categories that are underspent will probably be cut in next year's budget. Public sector salaries are not tied to profits, but to the size of the organization's budget.

Libraries that have an effective public relations program usually can secure the funding that they need to do a credible job. If the library is sold as a valuable community good, people will begin to equate it with the self esteem of the community. Libraries that are under the control of a parent political body will usually find that politicians will tend to put libraries low on the totem pole of political preferences. The taxpayers, fortunately, do not. Whenever libraries have the ability to bypass the politicians and appeal directly to the taxpayers for support, that level of support has been more than adequate. In community after community, throughout the United States, taxpayers have vigorously protested any cuts in library services and have often voted to override tax cutting initiatives, such as California's Proposition 13, in order to allow increased funding for libraries.

The industrial age is on the wane. We are in the information age and the librarians seem to be among the last to realize that fact and all it entails. They seem to understand that the library is a place to organize, store and retrieve information, but they are far short of understanding how to accomplish this goal with a high degree of efficiency in response to the demands of the library's consumers. Public librarians confuse their roles either with those of university librarians or with those of educational bureaucrats who are better at telling the public what's good for them than at responding to the needs of the public. So here again enters the "B" Factor; how can seemingly intelligent people come to such dumb conclusions? Let us now examine some of the ways that the "B" Factor can be eliminated.

3. What Does the Customer Pay the Library to Do?

"There is no such thing as darkness;
only a failure to see"
—Malcolm Muggeridge

For the most part, the taxpayers don't have any better idea of what the library should be doing than do the librarians who run the library. Libraries are still saddled with the stereotypical image of the library and the librarian. The library is merely a nice quiet place to read or do some research for a school assignment. If you need some help, ask the old lady at the reference desk, when she's not too busy telling people to be quiet. Maybe she can even recommend a good mystery.

In many places this stereotype is changing, but not rapidly enough. The "B" Factor causes bureaucrat librarians to deal with bureaucrat trustees in order to arrive at committee decisions which are usually long in coming and not responsive to the true needs of the library's customers. If leaders, the library entrepreneurs were instead permitted to make the marketing decisions, the library will be more able to respond rapidly and effectively to the changing needs of its market.

In actuality, the customers have little idea of what services a public library can provide for them. Each consumer requires something different from the library, and those needs constantly change depending on such things as time, circumstance, and technological developments. How could a library plan on offering video cassettes as a service before they were even invented? That's one of the reasons long range planning is often such a failure. It fails to take into account technological changes and locks the planner into an inflexible plan. Libraries, like businesses, must develop mechanisms to respond to consumer demand. What they usually have instead is a service program and collection of materials that are largely determined by a committee composed of the library hierarchy, who usually have the least contact with the public.

The librarians in contact with the public are often different from the librarians making the purchasing and service decisions. This is especially true in the larger libraries. As a general rule, the larger the library, the more out of touch with consumer demand are the people with the power to respond to that demand. What is needed is a mechanism through which the demands of the consumers can be channeled to those that have the power to respond to those demands. Better yet, the librarians who actually have direct contact with the members of the public should be given the authority to respond to their needs.

In even the smallest of libraries, which may have only a few professionals, the power of those librarians to rapidly and efficiently respond to the demands of the library's patrons is often sorely lacking. This is in no small part the result of the abysmally poor training afforded most public librarians. To make matters worse, the library profession, because of low pay and incorrect perceptions of the work actually done by public librarians, tends to attract people of lower quality than are needed. The library profession, like the education profession, tends to attract the type of people who are prone to become educational bureaucrats. These are the people who propose to do for the public what they think is good for them, regardless of what the public thinks.

Public libraries are not like any other tax supported services. They do not have a captive clientele. People don't have to use public libraries. They use them if the library provides services that are needed. Public libraries must develop a service program that recognizes the unique nature of library service. It must respond to consumer demand and provide services that attract customers. What public libraries need in leadership positions are business people trained and skilled in responding to the needs of their constituents, in an efficient and cost effective manner. Public librarians must never lose sight of the fact that they must attract their customers. If they fully understand the implications of this unique role, then libraries will be far ahead of other government agencies in gaining tax support for their services.

Too often, libraries wait at the end of the line for the leftovers of the funds given to other services that politicians consider more important. It's time to stop apologizing for spending tax money the way public schools have been doing for the last few decades. Libraries that provide quality services have to aggressively seek increased funding. Librarians can and will be in a better position to receive necessary funding when they better understand what their customers are willing to pay for, and when they are able to provide those services in the most cost effective manner possible.

4. What Is the Value to the Customer of the Library's Products?

What is truly amazing about the public's perception of the value of public libraries is that no matter what the current tax climate, the public loves its public libraries. John Berry wrote in a *Library Journal* article entitled "The Best Bargain in Town":

> ...a carefully executed sampling of library patrons, reminds us of decades of reports from public libraries everywhere in the U.S. Citizens loved their public libraries, and if that's no surprise, they apparently love them whether or not they are regular users. Our first discovery of this phenomena came decades ago when we stood outside city hall in Newark, New Jersey, as thousands of angry citizens packed a meeting of the City Council at which a proposal to close Newark's venerable Public Library was under debate. We asked every arriving citizen we could reach, when they had last been inside that library. Few had made a visit in years, yet all were ready to do committed battle to keep the institution open. They won the battle.
>
> More than two-thirds of the voters of Berkeley, California, voted to tax themselves to support their libraries at better than past levels, right on the heels of the tax revolt and the infamous Proposition 13. Near the height of the City's fiscal crisis, the voters of Cleveland repeatedly passed bond issues to support their public library. New York's erstwhile mayor, Abe Beame, received more letters supporting the New York Public Library, when a few of that library's branches were threatened, than he received about any municipal service during those times of fiscal crisis in New York. . . . [other] librarians reported equally high levels of satisfaction and support from the citizens they serve, and often those citizens added that they would be happy to pay more for library service!
>
> ...Public libraries are possibly the best bargain in the United States. Library support has ranged from one to two percent of U.S. municipal budgets for a century, rarely reaching the full two percent. For that comparative pittance, libraries know they serve about 25 percent of the population on a regular basis, and a much larger percentage less frequently. Very

few agencies, public or private, can claim to provide that much service. We don't know of any that do it on a shoestring and still manage to deliver satisfaction at the rate of 95 percent.

The point is that public libraries do an amazing job for very little money. Rather than apologize for the 25 percent who regularly use the library, we should be proud of it. Rather than apologize for the cost of that service, we should suggest that the cost per user or per taxpayer be compared with any other municipal service. Rather than be hesitant about tapping the resulting reservoir of citizen support, we should publicize it, nurture it, and make sure no elected officials forget it. Those libraries that have faced fiscal crises have learned that the citizens are on their side, and in the few unfortunate cases where the question was survival, they have survived and even been strengthened. The tax revolt, which is still with us, is not a library revolt. There is ample evidence that the taxes they pay for libraries are among the few taxes that citizens recognize as valid and necessary. If the reports from Wichita, Berkeley, Cleveland, New York, and thousands of other U.S. communities are any indication, public libraries fare better when they tap this vast reservoir of citizen support. These citizens are voters! In times like these, no politician at any level of government should be allowed to forget it. Public libraries are one of the few bargains left in America, and possibly the only bargain in municipal government.

In spite of this overwhelming support by taxpayers, libraries have generally missed their chances for greatly increased funding by not expanding their services to new markets, aggressively marketing their new and improved products and services, and then vigorously pursuing increased support for this increased service. They instead, beg for adequate funding, which rarely comes, and then use the lack of funding as an excuse for poor service. The "B" Factor has transformed all too many public library administrators into ordinary government bureaucrats who are loath to compete aggressively with their brethren from other agencies. That is why municipal libraries are often at the bottom of the list for increased funding and at the top of the list when municipal cuts are needed. They have failed to convince the politicians of their value and they have been funded accordingly. Only the librarian as leader-entrepreneur will be able to break this cycle of apology, negativism, and self-pity.

5. The Librarian as Entrepreneur

"Think Small. Big Ideas Upset Everyone"
—A sign on a leader's desk

Even with the varying types of library bureaucratic organizations, creative and imaginative library leaders can function as virtual library entrepreneurs. Nothing less than that is satisfactory, if this profession is truly going to achieve excellence. We need to be supply-side librarians, if there is such a thing. The question that this profession has to ask is the age old one, "What came first, the chicken or the egg?"

Economists have labored over their graphs and mathematical calculations in attempts to prove whether demand creates supply or supply creates demand. Is there a market that the entrepreneur feels a need to fill, or does he create a market for his product? In this aspect, bureaucrat librarians make the same mistake as all other governmental planners. They assume they are filling the needs of their customers. They sit in their ivory towers and decide what services are "useful and needed" by their clientele. Much like their brethren in the educational community, they are highly unsuccessful in their ability to accurately gauge the depth and breadth of their markets.

Most citizens have a very limited view of what a public library is supposed to be doing. Besides the negative effects of the stereotypical image held by the general public, librarians have failed to recognize that library service is actually a fragmented series of various markets. Library service is different things to different people. It satisfies the individual if it fulfills a particular need. The customer often doesn't recognize what that particular need is. Most people who don't use the public library don't do so because it doesn't provide a service the individual wants, or because the individual isn't aware that the library does, in fact, provide such a service.

It is the library director as librarian-entrepreneur, who through his or her innovative and creative efforts must not only respond to the

18

perceived needs of each individual consumer, but must also create markets for new library services. The library bureaucrat follows traditional patterns and relies heavily on time consuming and cumbersome committee decisions before introducing and implementing new services. The librarian-entrepreneur experiments, and takes risks. He or she learns through trial and error, and in doing so is better able to respond to consumer demand and to create and develop new markets and new services. He or she also always keeps a keen eye on improving and making more efficient traditional library services.

The library market is, in actuality, made up of the needs, whether realized or not, that each individual potential user can have. Although today's public libraries are held in high esteem by 95 percent of the populace, they are not utilized by nearly that percentage. In spite of the monopoly power of the public library, most public libraries attract only about 30 percent of their potential market. Everyone may love the library, but not everyone uses it. It is the job of the librarian-entrepreneur to increase that percentage of use, by truly making the library responsive to the needs of its constituents.

This goal brings to mind the economists' tale of two shoe salesmen who were sent to a remote Third World country. One called the main office and complained to the boss that there was no market for his product here. The custom was to go barefoot. The other salesman called the factory and asked them to increase production. "People without shoes need them," he said. "They just don't know it yet." Librarian-bureaucrats often fail to recognize the need to create markets, and that is in large part the reason that many librarians are prone to developing services and collections that are little used, while being loath to provide popular, heavily utilized services, such as a sufficient number of best sellers, romance novels, detective stories or video cassettes.

As George Gilder wrote in the *Spirit of Enterprise*, in 1984,

> Still, one of the key principles of entrepreneurship—the business of breaking the settled mold—is the absence of clear and fast rules. Some successful entrepreneurs, following in the footsteps of Andrew Carnegie, a man famously ignorant in the technology of steel, have launched companies in fields they have little understood. Carnegie explained his achievement in a suggested epitaph. "Here lies a man who knew how to gather around him men who were more clever than himself."
> ...Entrepreneurs can be pompous and vain where it doesn't count; but in their own enterprise, the first law is to listen. They must be meek enough and shrewd enough to endure the humbling eclipse of self that comes of profound learning from others.

In the history of enterprise, most of the protagonists of major new products and companies began their education—and discovered the secrets of their later breakthroughs—not in the classroom, where the old ways were taught, but in the factories and labs where the new ways are wrought.

. . . Because [the entrepreneur] started in rebellion against established firms, he bears a natural skepticism towards the settled enterprise. Because he had to make scores of decisions before all the information was in, he recognizes that the enterprise always consists of action in uncertainty. The entrepreneur prevails, not by understanding an existing situation in all its complex particulars, but by creating a new situation which others must try to comprehend. The enterprise is an aggressive action, not a reaction. When it is successfully launched, all the rest of society—government, labor, other businesses—will have to react. In a sense, entrepreneurship is the creation of surprise. It entails breaking the looking glass of established ideas—even the gleaming mirrors of executive suites—and stepping into the often greasy and fetid bins of creation.

In the entrepreneur's contrarian domains, he needs most of all a willingness to accept failure, learn from it, and act boldly in the shadow of doubt. He inhabits a realm where the last becomes the first, where supply creates demand, where belief precedes knowledge. It is a world where expertise may be a form of ignorance and the best possibilities spring from the consensus of impossibility. It is a world where service of others—solving their problems and taking on new ones for yourself—is the prime source of leadership and wealth.

It was not until I studied economics at the tender age of thirty-five, that I realized that I was actually a librarian-entrepreneur. When I was but twenty-nine years old, I was given the opportunity to become the director of a library serving a middle class community of 50,000 people. The library was quartered in an old one room wooden house, and stocked with only a few thousand hand-me-down books. The board of trustees were very political and overly involved in the library's day to day operations. The only thing about this place that resembled a public library was its name. This institution was stuck in the mud, going nowhere fast.

At this point, its one saving grace was that the majority of the trustees realized the dire shape that the library was in and were determined to do something about it. This was evidenced in that they swallowed their pride and hired a brash young fellow like me, even though they must have sensed that their political power would never be the same.

My predecessors were basically the cheapest things that money could buy. They were perfect examples of the age old adage, "you get what you pay for." While libraries in surrounding communities were flourishing—new buildings, expanded services, etc.—this institution was dead in the water. The director who preceded me was a mere figurehead, who spent most of his time avoiding a few nit-picking trustees who based their evaluations of him on gossip from members of the staff who had gotten their jobs through friendship with certain trustees, rather than through merit. Civil service rules were blatantly ignored and the majority of library employment was nothing more than political patronage. This poor guy was on the carpet at every board meeting, forced to constantly defend himself against the most trivial of perceived infractions. I think that it was a great shock to the trustees that even this lowly director, who they had constantly criticized as little more than an inept bumbling fool, had actually been able to find other employment. They had mistakenly assumed that he could absorb abuse ad infinitum.

The majority of the board, albeit a small one, had apparently realized that a drastic change was needed. The climate was ripe for someone like me. I was young and aggressive, and possessed qualifications not normally found amongst librarians. I had served as a Military Police officer in the U.S. Army, and had also served as a Special Agent of the F.B.I. In the initial interview I was proud to stress my minimal knowledge of librarianship and my natural gift for leadership, which was enhanced by my military training. I was obviously not the classic librarian-bureaucrat that they had learned to expect, but I got the job anyway. They must have figured, "What the heck! We've tried people from the group that we were expected to hire from. Now, let's give this odd-ball a chance."

Once I began, I found the job to be very challenging indeed. Was this really an advancement in my career? I had given up a relatively safe tenured civil service position for an insecure one. In my new position, I was not tenured and could be fired, without cause, at any time during a six month probationary period. I had no contract. My board was composed entirely of blue collar workers, whose highest level of educational achievement was high school. They displayed a pronounced anti-education bias. This is one of the reasons that I had to take a cut in salary from my last position to get the job. From their point of view, they couldn't understand how a mere librarian could be worth my asking price. We negotiated and I lost. I not only took less salary, but had no health insurance coverage.

I thought that I must be doing something basically wrong. In private industry, I thought talented people were sought after. They were offered attractive salary and fringe benefit packages. Not so in the library business. Here I was taking a job at a cut in pay and no health plan—no small consideration, as I had two toddlers and a third child on the way. I didn't even have an office. I had to renovate an old closet that was approximately three feet by four feet, which was to serve as an extremely cramped office for the next two years. It was actually as if they thought they were doing me a favor by hiring me. As it turned out later, they were. I had taken a big risk, but in return I had been given the opportunity to create something from nothing. This library would never be the same again.

Today, the Middle Country Public Library is the biggest and busiest library on Long Island. It serves approximately 55,000 residents and has achieved circulation figures of over 925,000 per year, a figure never before reached by any Long Island public library, regardless of the size of the population served. We boast a yearly materials budget of over $1 million, and devote approximately 50 percent of our operating budget to salaries, while paying salaries that are among the highest in the industry. We do this by employing a highly motivated, well paid, but very small staff. That's service and efficiency in action.

In addition to this, we boast an innovative and extensive array of unique services, such as career counseling, a computer training center, a Parent/Child Workshop, and a Family Resource Information Center. Many of these special programs are held at our satellite facility, which we like to call our Cultural Center. We are especially proud of our Parent/Child Workshop, which was created and developed by our staff. This popular program was not developed as the result of a committee or a survey. We perceived a need. We tried it. People liked it, so we did more of it. This program has now been replicated by many libraries throughout not only Long Island, but the United States and Europe (an article on this innovative program can be found in the April 1985 issue of *School Library Journal*).

I had virtually invented this library; created it out of almost nothing. I had been successful, primarily because I have always looked upon the nature of my job as one of leadership, not management. I attempted to create an atmosphere that would encourage and enhance the creative talents of the people who worked for me. From my previous work experience I had already developed quite a distaste for the ways of bureaucrats.

I had never thought that my function was to follow established patterns. I was always questioning, wondering if there were ways to do it faster and better. I wanted to invent new ways of doing things. Most of what was taught in library school was so much bunk. Let's figure out what services we should be offering and then let's figure out how to provide them most rapidly and most efficiently. That was my credo. It was not until I undertook the study of economics, though, that I realized that I was actually a librarian-entrepreneur. The talents of many of our colleagues are wasted because they haven't arrived at that realization.

John Lukas, in a 1984 article in *U.S. News and World Report*, writes:

> Two hundred years after its birth, the United States has been unable to avoid the degeneration of some of its institutions.
>
> The main source of this decay is the rise of bureaucracy and of the bureaucratic mind. The inclination to administer, to standardize, to regulate, to reorganize, to define—and therefore constrict—personal activity and private choice is endemic in so called private institutions, corporations, businesses as much as in public ones.
>
> Bureaucratization is constricting not only our channels of production, but those of our intellectual commerce. . . . Now the relatively uneducated and half educated often express themselves in long words and surrealistic abstractions.
>
> Bureaucratic language, by its very nature, is abstract, lengthy and vague, wherefore an awful lot of things in this country are now couched in abstractions. This is not merely a matter of esthetics or of linguistic purity; it reflects a now widespread sluggishness of mind. The pace at which ideas move—the process whereby even the most reasonable ideas are translated into practice—is disturbingly slow and complex—and often impossible.
>
> Large numbers of people adapt their entire personalities to the bureaucratic system—or lack of system. This is true in almost every field of life, from politics to publishing, from art criticism to corporate business.

It is this tendency to slide so easily into the bureaucratic mold, combined with the failure of librarians to view themselves as librarian-entrepreneurs, that activates the "B" Factor. By learning the ways of the bureaucracy instead of those of leadership, otherwise reasonable, intelligent people, tend to behave in a manner that could aptly be described as foolish or just plain dumb. We have to fight the system. We have to change the system. We must not become a part of it.

6. Barriers to Innovation

"Whenever anything is being accomplished anywhere,
it is being done by a monomaniac with a mission "
—Peter Drucker

Peter Drucker is one of America's leading exponents of the management principles that I am applying to public library administration in this book. In his work, *Innovation and Entrepreneurship*, he discusses public institutions. Drucker believes that all institutions, policies, products, services, and the like outlive their usefulness and become obsolete. Sustaining the obsolete is a drain on resources which is counterproductive for the economic good of society. Libraries, like most other public institutions, are slow to innovate because they keep trying to do the same old things better. When new services, programs and procedures are instituted, they are often done so after a long bureaucratic process, involving lengthy committee meetings, consultants' reports, and management elitism. Change occurs, but slowly, and is often too little and too late.

Drucker's concepts are based on his theory that change is normal and healthy. He views the primary goal of business (this includes the library business) as doing something different rather than doing something better that is already being done. The only constant is the inevitability of change. We can either nurture it or we can hinder it. Drucker says the need to innovate in public service organizations is crucial, but nonetheless difficult because of certain barriers.

Drucker identifies the first barrier as the fact that public institutions base their operation on a budget rather than being paid out of results. Success is most often defined by obtaining a larger budget rather than by obtaining results. Library bureaucrats are rewarded by enlarging their staffs, their budgets, and their scope of operations, not by the efficiency of their operations and the suitability and quality of the services they offer to the public. Library services are often budget

24

driven; i.e., they are limited by the estimates placed in the various budget categories, rather than having consumer demand determine the amounts that are budgeted for various services. There are libraries, for example, that don't have enough money to buy books sufficient to meet the demand of their customers, simply because they have not effectively gauged consumer demand, and therefore didn't budget enough money. Consumer demand should be the prime factor in deciding how much funding goes into each of the library's budget categories. Often it is the other way around. The needs of the consumers are not met because of budget limitations. That's backwards.

Drucker considers the next barrier to innovation to be the fact that public service institutions depend on a multitude of constituents, rather than a share of the market. Libraries, for example, tend to feel that everyone must be satisfied, and that the institution can't afford to alienate anyone. Libraries actually do serve a multitude of fragmented markets. People are attracted to, and use the public library for, a wide variety of reasons. The question that library leaders are faced with is not only what services should be offered, but to whom, and to what extent should those services be offered. These are difficult decisions for a political institution. All too often, services are offered because of political pressures rather than consumer demand. The more that you are able to run your library like a business and the less like a political institution, the better off everyone will be. Your guiding principle should always be to strive to respond to consumer demand rather than political pressure. Bureaucrats will do the opposite. It's the same for other political entities. Roads don't always get built where they are most needed, but rather in the regions that are able to apply the most political muscle.

The next barrier to innovation, according to Drucker, is that public service institutions are perceived as existing to do good. Their missions are often viewed as moral absolutes, rather than economic in nature and subject to cost-benefit analysis. Public service is, in fact, something people buy. The difference is that in the market system consumers have free choice as to where to spend their dollars, while in the political system payment for services is extracted through taxes. Failure to achieve objectives which the library administration perceives as good usually results in increased efforts and funding, even though the service in question may be used by only a handful of people. Public service institutions try to maximize, rather than optimize, and a goal of maximization can never be obtained. The concept of scarcity decrees that although the wants and needs of society are unlimited, the resources of society are limited. The same is true for the public library.

This cannot be figured out on a Lotus spreadsheet. It is an art. It is not a science. It requires intelligent judgment, risk taking, and above all, constant contact with the staff and the members of the public. We cannot offer only those services that are the cheapest and most efficient to administer. If that were the case, all public libraries would have nothing but videos and junk paperbacks. Services must be viewed on a cost-benefit basis. Services that are very expensive and benefit only a few must be eliminated. Some services, for example, such as talking books for the blind, cannot totally be judged on a cost-benefit basis. Services such as these should be offered no matter what the cost, although library administrators should seek to deliver those services as efficiently as possible, and should not be afraid to seek alternative new services if costs can be reduced by using those alternatives. Even when you feel that you have a moral imperative to offer a service regardless of its costs, there is still room for innovation.

Ivory tower library directors love to provide services that look good on their resumes, or about which they can write papers for library publications, regardless of whether those services truly meet the needs of their constituents. Library leaders are constantly reviewing their service programs to see what needs to be modified, eliminated or added. Listen to your staff. Listen to your public. If it seems that enough people want a service and are using it, then provide it. Thomas Edison once said, "I failed my way to success." We learn by making mistakes, and learning from those mistakes is a great way to innovate, grow and change. It is cheaper and better to try and fail, than to spend the time studying whether failure is possible. The library business is already overcrowded with bureaucratic elitists who think that only they know what is best for the public and the staff. Run your library like a business, and innovate, innovate, innovate. Your public and your staff will love what you are doing for them. You will be a librarian-entrepreneur, rather than a librarian-bureaucrat. You'll be what Tom Peters calls "that persistent champion" who is the driving force behind anything that is getting done anywhere.

7. Implementing Your Ideas

"They said it couldn't be done.
But they're not always right"
—Casey Stengel

In order to implement your ideas, it must first be assumed that you have some. This is not always the case in the bureaucratic organization. Bureaucrats will slavishly adhere to existing patterns and methods. This is not exactly a fertile breeding ground for new and innovative ideas. Bureaucrats tend to like the status quo. It gives them a nice safe and secure feeling.

Librarian-entrepreneurs, on the other hand, are a constant source of new ideas. They realize that the inevitability of change is the only constant. They are always seeking new markets for their services, creating a variety of services that most people never thought would be done by a public library. They are also constantly challenging the way the profession is practiced. What is the role of the reference librarian, the children's librarian, the AV librarian? Should these positions continue to exist in their present form? Should they be modified, or eliminated? Challenging the established norms is the main function of the librarian-entrepreneur.

People often cling slavishly to old methods without ever questioning why things are done, or if there is a better way to do them. Remember the old story about the mother who was baking a ham for dinner? Her daughter asked her why she always cut the end off the ham before placing it in the oven. She replied that she had always done it that way, because she had learned from her mother and her mother always cut the end off the ham. Both women then turned to the grandmother and finally asked why she had cut the end off the ham before cooking it. The grandmother replied, "Because the pan I had was too small and I always had to cut the end off to make it fit."

One of the great innovations in the workplace today is the changing

27

nature of work. Technology is changing the way things are done. Innovators are constantly looking for new and better ways to provide service to their customers. They realize that the needs of their client base are constantly changing. New services must be tried, and old services must be improved. If you follow the traditional bureaucratic method of trying to implement your ideas, you will have great difficulty in achieving your aims, and your achievements, to a large degree, will be watered-down versions of your original ideas. Be prepared also for the enormous time lag between the conception of an idea and its actual implementation. What is most shocking about this whole procedure is that bureaucrats accept as normal this time consuming and stultifying process.

Here's how the process will work in a typical bureaucratic organization:

1. Ideas for new services or for improvements in existing services only get to see the light of day if they are the brainchild of a high level library official. This usually will be the library director, a board member, or a department head. Let's suppose, for the purposes of this illustration, that one of these folks has gotten the idea to start a circulating collection of video cassettes.

2. This idea is not discussed with any staff members who are in direct contact with the public.

3. The idea is tossed around among the director and several other high level officials to see if it is considered worthy for presentation to the board of trustees.

4. The next step is to form a committee, which will study the merits of the idea.

5. If the idea is of a great enough magnitude, a consultant may be called in to provide for a more in-depth study of the matter. If the bureaucrats are really good at this, the consultants will know as little about this newly proposed service as the people on the committee. This is especially true if this is a completely new service. Who would know much about circulating video cassettes in a public library, if no one has actually done it before?

The people who would be in the best position to provide the most reliable information about the viability of this new service, the customers, and the staff members who are in direct contact with the customers, have yet to be consulted.

6. The committee will then review all the material collected and make a report to the director. The director will then review all the

material and decide whether or not to make a recommendation to the board of trustees. During this process, a considerable amount of time will have elapsed. No service has been introduced and the customers have not had the use of even one video cassette.

7. At this point, let us assume that the director has decided that this project does merit board consideration. So far, decisions regarding the feasibility of offering this service have been left entirely in the hands of bureaucrats who profess to know what library patrons need and want, yet have little or no contact with them. The "B" Factor has taken hold and has been a major influence in determining whether this service will be offered to the public or not. So-called professionals, aided by consultants, have used a flawed mechanism to reach a decision about what they think should be done.

8. After lengthy delays, a watered down version of what could be possible, is added to next year's budget, to be implemented later.

This process can be even more time consuming and less responsive than as described here, depending on the pomposity of the bureaucrats and the layers of bureaucracy with which the participants must deal. The more professionals, the more consultants, the more committees, the more governmental agencies, and the more sources of funding that must be involved in the process, the less likely it will be that this project will come to fruition in any reasonable amount of time; although this is difficult to judge, because in the world of the bureaucrat the unreasonable is often accepted as the norm.

The key thing to note here, is that while this enormous volume of activity is going on, nothing is really happening. There is a great difference between action and motion. What we have here is much motion, the main function of which has been to generate reams of paperwork. All the people involved are convinced that the effort they have expended has been completely worthwhile. What actually has happened is that little of anything has happened, especially anything that could reasonably be viewed as productive. This idea has still not been translated in the most efficient and rapid manner into a service that is being utilized by the library's customers.

Now let's take a look at how to de-bureaucratize this situation:

1. An idea to begin a circulating video cassette collection is born. This could come from any level within the organization. The idea could have come from a customer, or some bright staff member just might have thought that this would be something that the customers might go for.

2. No matter where the idea originated, there should be an efficient mechanism in place to facilitate its implementation. It must get to the person with the power to implement it as rapidly as possible. This process may involve no more than a discussion between the person who had the idea and the director. Every person who might know how to deliver this service should be allowed input in to this discussion. This is best accomplished in the most informal manner possible. Those who are skillful practitioners of MBWA (Management By Wandering Around; see Chapter 14), will already be adept at this.

3. After the person with the power to implement this idea has received sufficient information, a decision is made. This procedure should take hours or days, not weeks, months or years. Either scrap the idea or go ahead with it. Notice that there are no committee reports, feasibility studies, consultants' reports or any other such nonsense. Decision making and implementation are swift. We learn through our mistakes. It is cheaper and faster to try and fail, than to study whether failure is possible.

This sounds easy, but it seems obvious that most people aren't in a position where this will work. If that's what you think, then you don't understand anything about leadership. This is not about what most people can't do. It is about leadership. It is about the few people who are smart enough and brave enough to function as leaders. Of course this can't work if you assume that you're only going to function within the existing bureaucratic structure. Leadership involves not accepting bureaucracy, but of constantly striving to make basic changes in how bureaucracy operates. Less bureaucratic motion and more action should be the goal, and a mechanism should be established to facilitate that end.

One way of implementing new programs rapidly would be for the library to have a research and development fund which could be used to fund experimental programs. One person, either the director or a major department head, would have the authority to approve use of these funds, thus eliminating layers of bureaucracy. If the program was successful, it could be expanded. If it needed modification, then that could be done. Again, action, not motion is what is desired.

In the long run, it is faster and cheaper to try, fail, and learn from failure, than to spend the time and money studying, ad infinitum, whether trying something will result in failure or success. It is by trying and failing that we first learned, and it is through this method that we still learn the most. This is the world of the entrepreneur, in which we gain the experience necessary to make speedy decisions about whether services should be added, eliminated, expanded, contracted, or modified in any other way. There must be a constant process of trial and error. We must have a burning desire to do it better and more efficiently. This takes the vision and courage of the entrepreneur; not common commodities in the average bureaucracy.

If you try circulating video cassettes, you'll find out soon enough whether people want to use them. You will be responding to consumer demand, not from an ivory tower, but through trial and error. This is not pie in the sky. It can be done. It has been done.

Video cassettes propose a clear illustration of the entrepreneurial vs. the bureaucratic process. They were first introduced by a few libraries on Long Island in the late 1970s, when most people had never heard of video cassettes. These libraries were the first in the country to introduce this service, because they sensed a potential market and decided to test it. They simply believed that this might be something people would like, so they tried it. The service didn't really take off until the 1980s, when the price of video recorders dropped dramatically and the selection of tapes increased sharply. By this time, these entrepreneurial libraries already had this service in place. As it became more popular, they simply expanded and developed it. It wasn't difficult because they already had spent years working all the bugs out. Other libraries were just beginning to discuss the possibility of instituting this service and, as a result, were many years behind those libraries with the courage and foresight to try something new. There are still lengthy debates going on about the size and compositions of the video tape collections in other libraries.

The leaders who tried this had no such problems, because they found out what people wanted and got it fast. While other library-bureaucracies generated lots of talk and paperwork, customers of entrepreneurial libraries have enjoyed using large and versatile video cassette collections. This highly popular service has turned out to be one of the most cost effective of all library services. While others were studying, these libraries were serving. They had tapped a whole new marketplace of customers. To these librarian-entrepreneurs, the customer is king, and the results of that attitude speak for themselves.

If you or someone you know has an idea, LISTEN, and if experience and common sense tells you that it might be worthwhile, give it a try; DO IT... and if it doesn't work exactly like you thought, then change it and do it again. Your goal should always be to have the shortest time span possible between the origination of an idea and the implementation of that idea.

8. Productivity: What It Is and How to Achieve It

*"Running a business is 95 percent
people and 5 percent economics"*
—**Anonymous**

Sometimes it seems that people view productivity as simply working harder. Additional action does not necessarily guarantee increased productivity. People often spend time "spinning their wheels" without actually producing very much. A quick lesson in economics should help you to better understand the nature of the productive process. Underlying the debate about all economic issues is one basic economic problem. People cannot have everything they want, neither in goods nor in services. There is never enough to satisfy everyone. Therefore, scarcity is inevitable. Whenever there is scarcity, people disagree about priorities. An understanding of the concept of the inevitability of scarcity is as vital in determining library services as it is in determining how we satisfy all of our other needs and wants. Self interest enters into everyone's opinions. This concept of scarcity is difficult for many Americans to accept. We are the richest most powerful nation in the world. We produce so much that we are running out of space to dispose of all the waste we create. How can we say there is scarcity? The answer is that scarcity exists because of two conditions: (1) Productive capacity is limited. (2) Wants are unlimited.

Satisfying people's wants and needs begins with unprocessed resources. The resources that go into making products are called factors of production. These resources are grouped into four categories: land, labor, capital and entrepreneurship. Noneconomists usually refer to resources as natural resources, something that exists apart from people. In economic terms, however, a resource may also be a person or a good produced by human labor.

    1. Land. To the economist, land means more than real estate.

Land refers to every natural resource: water, air, sunshine, vegetation, wild animals, and deposits of minerals.

2. Capital. To the layman, capital means simply money. To an economist, capital refers to manmade resources that are not consumed, but are used to create or transport other products. Some examples of capital resources would be factories, machinery, railroads and highways. Knowing the difference between capital goods and consumer goods is crucial to understanding economics. Consumer goods, whether they be washing machines or hamburgers, are consumed, while capital goods remain, turning out more and more products.

3. Labor. Labor encompasses virtually all human skills, both physical and mental, which can be used in producing goods and services.

4. Entrepreneurship. Before products can be made from resources, someone needs to discover the resources, invent a production process, or create a business. The functions of organizing, directing, and managing the factors of production are performed by the entrepreneur. Like other factors of production, entrepreneurship is in scarce supply. It is not a common talent, and not everyone who has it chooses to use it.

Some qualified people are reluctant to use their entrepreneurial talent because of one special function of the entrepreneur—risk taking. There is no guarantee that risks will be rewarded. In the public sector, entrepreneurship is rare because the public sector tends to attract the type of people who are risk averse. These are people who seek civil service jobs because of the security involved. Others, who find that they do have entrepreneurial abilities, may be discouraged from using them because of the lack of adequate rewards for doing so in the public sector. The main goal in the public sector is often merely to NOT make a mistake. Public sector bureaucrats are often punished severely for mistakes and are rarely rewarded adequately for taking risks that result in increased productivity or better services. The less one does in the public sector, the less chance there is of making a mistake. Often, the less efficient bureaucrats are more highly rewarded because it takes more resources to accomplish their goals, and that often means that they will be heading a larger bureaucracy, and thus spending more taxpayer money. The size of a bureaucracy is often the yardstick used to determine their compensation. This is exactly the opposite of the motivation to be efficient caused by the profit motive in the private sector.

Understanding economics also involves understanding the idea of economizing—of allocating the limited material resources of society in such a way that inevitably scarce goods and services are produced and distributed in a way that best satisfies the needs and wants of society. Economics, therefore, can be defined as the social science which studies the problem of using scarce resources to satisfy society's unlimited wants. Faced with the dilemma of limited products and unlimited wants and needs, we must make choices. The inevitability of scarcity leads directly to the inevitability of choice. How are the resources to be used? What products should be made with the limited resources? In what quantity? Who should get them?

The necessity to make choices is a concept that is not only essential to understanding how economics affects society as a whole, but in understanding the process involved in making public policy decisions concerning public library services. What services should be offered? What quality should they be? Who gets to use them? What is their benefit to the individual and to the community as a whole? Where should they be offered? How much should they cost and who should pay? These are just a few of the decisions that must be made by library directors on an ongoing basis. An understanding of economics and the productive process is essential if intelligent choices are to be made. Too often, this is just a haphazard procedure, influenced by the self-interest of bureaucrats, politicians, and pressure groups.

Factors of Production

Natural Resources
Labor
Capital   Product or Service
Entrepreneur

Factors of Production (Library Service)

Natural resources (paper, fuel oil, etc.)
Labor (librarians, clerks, pages, custodians)
Capital (library buildings and property)   Library Service
Entrepreneur (library director)

Since needs and wants for products are unlimited and resources are limited, it would be self-defeating to waste resources by producing goods in any but the most efficient way. When determining how to make a product, society should attempt to use the fewest possible resources to obtain a given level of output. It should also attempt to achieve the greatest output from a given level of resources. We should also attempt to satisfy the needs and wants of society, using the fewest possible resources to obtain the highest level of output possible. This is known as technological efficiency. If we succeed in being technologically efficient, every available resource is being used. Complete technological efficiency is a goal that we always strive to reach, but, in fact, never do.

Technological efficiency alone is not enough, however. The productive process is essentially useless if it produces something no one wants. Resources must be allocated to the production of goods and services that people want. If the economy produces the combination of goods and services that is consistent with society's economic goals, it has achieved allocative efficiency. In a market economy, such as ours, consumer sovereignty is the guiding principle. What products will be made is decided by consumer demand, and the force that maintains demand is consumer satisfaction with the process. Consumers demand those products that best satisfy their needs and wants, and the economic system responds to supply them. Of course, the free enterprise system isn't that simple and certainly doesn't run that smoothly, but those are the basic principles involved in the determination of what, for whom and how much is produced.

The situation is quite different in providing services through the government sector. Politics, not consumer sovereignty, is the guiding force. Government services, such as a public library, are provided because a pure market system would not produce enough public goods. This is because of the nature of public goods. If people can't be charged for using them on a per use basis, a free market would underproduce them. The result would be allocative inefficiency. If services such as police protection, national defenses, and library services are to be provided at the level that society desires, they must be provided through the government sector. Library services, like all other public services provided under a democratic form of government, are subject to debate on the level at which public goods should be provided and the methods used to pay for them. It is difficult to achieve allocative efficiency through the political process. The result is a series of compromises that those in political power find acceptable.

The public library is a unique public service in that it does not have a captive audience. People don't have to use the public library, as they would utilize police, fire or school services. People don't choose the fire department they think is most efficiently run, if their house is on fire. They must utilize the one chartered to serve their municipality. If the public library does not provide services that they find useful, they simply don't use it, or don't use it to the extent that it could be used. Sometimes people are offered some choice in this matter by being able to choose between libraries by utilizing different branches within the same system, or utilizing libraries in other communities through various reciprocal borrowing programs. This raises serious questions concerning who should pay for the various library resources, the tax-payers of the community in which the library is located, or the users of its services? Often the two are not the same.

Due to this unique feature of public libraries, they are in a position to market their services much like a private business. Public libraries often attempt to do this, and by doing so are getting as close as possible to providing the taxpayer with a degree of consumer sovereignty. The more the public library is able to operate like a private business and the less like a political institution, the more technologically efficient it will become.

One of the most common complaints about the government is that it is technologically inefficient. It throws people and money at its problems, and thus spends too much to accomplish a given task. Duplication, bureaucracy, red tape, and patronage are several of the reasons given for governmental inefficiency. This is because of a significant difference in the public and private sector—the absence of the profit motive. As a result, there is less incentive for the public sector to achieve technological efficiency. In the private sector, cost savings mean higher profits and increased rewards for management. In the public sector these rewards and incentives are absent. In fact, public officials who reduce costs would often be penalized for administering a smaller bureaucracy and often come under attack by unions for attempting to reduce the size of the work force.

The public library is a labor intensive business, as opposed to a capital intensive business. A capital intensive business is one in which natural resources and capital comprise a large portion of the cost of producing the product. The auto or steel industries, for example, are examples of capital intensive businesses. Labor is not the main cost of producing the product. If labor represents only 20 percent of the cost of producing an automobile, then changes in labor rates would only have an effect on 20 percent of the cost of the product. A school would be an example of a labor intensive business. Labor makes up the largest percentage of the cost of schooling. If you want to make significant increases in productivity in a labor intensive business, you must seek to reduce the cost of labor. This doesn't necessarily mean reducing salaries, but rather working with the smallest percentage of labor possible.

The public library is a labor intensive business that is particularly adaptive to increases in productivity. The business of the public library is to provide services for the entertainment and enlightenment of the public, and further to provide those services in the most efficient manner possible. The main way this is accomplished is through the storage and retrieval of information in all its various forms. Just as computers have caused great increases in productivity in office work, so can they cause great increases in productivity in the public library. What a computer basically does is to store and retrieve information. From billing, to payroll, to circulation control and the card catalog, the computer can be utilized in the public library in a manner that will increase service and decrease the library's reliance on many labor intensive procedures. If the library's annual labor costs are 70 percent of its total operating costs, then the largest increases in efficiency can come through reducing the percentage of this part of operating costs. To do this, libraries must have the capital necessary to invest in upgrading plant and equipment. Like many public facilities, libraries often find themselves saddled with politically short range decisions. Private businesses are far more likely to make needed capital improvements to stay competitive.

Discussions concerning the lack of technological efficiency in public libraries do not indicate that library employees are lazy or incompetent. It only means that there is less incentive to be efficient in the government than in the private sector. Public sector special interests actually work to increase costs in many areas. Translating good intentions into good library policy is not always easy. The library director is constantly required to walk the fine line of compromise between what is politically and economically wise.

9. Organizational Structure and Chain of Command

"So much of what we call management consists of making it difficult for people to work"
—Peter Drucker

One of the basics to running any organization is to have a clearly defined organizational structure which outlines the lines of authority. Libraries, like many organizations, tend to range to great extremes in this area. There are libraries that utilize lengthy and over complicated organizational charts, and there are those that have none at all. Neither extreme is desirable, because it is important for any organization to clearly define lines of authority and responsibility. When libraries, usually the larger ones, have an organizational chart that is so complicated that it cannot be relied upon to clarify the inner mechanisms that are the basis for the internal functions of the library, chaos is the usual result. The absence of an organizational chart, especially in the smaller libraries, is also not desirable, but will not cause nearly the problems that such a situation would cause in larger institutions.

In order for an organizational chart to be developed and effectively used, the library director should ask the same questions that apply when deciding to call a meeting or when deciding what and how many administrative forms are necessary to effectively conduct business: "Does this have a purpose, and if so, is this chart helping our library to realize that purpose?"

The organizational chart should be as simple as possible and it should clearly and concisely outline the lines of authority. Who is responsible for what, and who works for whom; these are the only reasons for organizational charts to exist. If this is not clear then you will not know who is responsible for accomplishing the library's various tasks, and worse, your personnel will be confused as to which supervisor they are supposedly responsible to.

A common mistake is to have no one in charge. This forces all channels of communication to the top, causes procedural overlaps, and severely delays the decision making and implementation processes. It is also obvious when this happens that, although titles may profess otherwise, no one is really in charge but the director. Sometimes this bureaucratic maelstrom gets to the level of the board of trustees, and if that happens, even the director isn't able to exercise executive authority. The director, in such a situation, goes to each board meeting with a laundry list of things to be done, and the trustees proceed to micromanage the library, usually through a committee structure.

The opposite of this is to have an organizational structure that seems to make sense on paper, but in reality is not generally observed. Each worker, in effect, has several bosses. For example, the custodian cleaning at night may report to the head custodian. The head custodian may report to the superintendent of buildings and grounds. The superintendent reports to the assistant director for business, who in turn reports to the associate director. Authority is not transmitted to the lower levels of employees, but rather maintained at the top. All of these supervisors may become involved with solving problems and giving instructions to the custodian. Their role usually is to collect data and pass them along to the director, associate director or the board of trustees. In this situation there are several people in charge, all giving conflicting orders, with no one really in charge, except the director. This demonstrates an important principle which must always be followed without exception:

The One Boss Only Rule. When there is more than one person to report to, no one is in charge. Everyone should have only one boss, and employees should deal only with their immediate boss. Having employees pulled several different ways, with conflicting orders, is not only inefficient, but will greatly damage morale and increase the level of employee frustration. Give your supervisors all the authority and support they need to do their work. Never vary from it. Your organization will crumble like a house of cards if you do.

There are an infinite number of organizational structures that can be utilized. Here is one example:

Organizational Chart

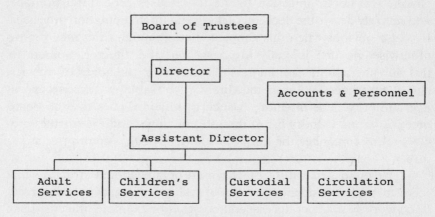

The Adult Services, Children's Services, Circulation Services and Custodial Services Departments all report to the Assistant Director, whose basic duties are to be in charge of the delivery of public services. Underneath each department head could be a variety of supervisory personnel assigned to different tasks.

This is just one example. You must develop a structure that best suits the needs of your library. The particular structure that you choose is not important. What is important is that certain basic guidelines be followed without exception. These are:

1. Keep it simple. Keep the layers of bureaucracy to a minimum. A simple rule to follow is, never create a title before the person does the job. This increases bureaucratic behavior. The more important sounding the title, the less work the person is likely to do. Let people develop their own job guidelines in accomplishing organizational goals, and then think of a descriptive title that will indicate what they are actually doing.

2. Every employee must have only one boss. Whatever the structure, each employee must report *only* to the supervisor directly above. If employees are allowed to bypass the chain of command and go around their supervisors to a higher level of authority, anarchy will result. If you don't believe this, just imagine how you would like it if employees you were assigned to supervise were able to take every minor complaint about you directly to your boss. Formal grievance procedures should be in place to deal with real injustices, but otherwise, the day to day operation of the library must be handled strictly by following the chain of command. NO EXCEPTIONS!

3. Don't place people in supervisory positions that have nothing else to do but supervise. These people will hinder the productive process with endless meetings and paperwork if their only function is to supervise others. Their main purpose will be to justify their own existence through a series of bureaucratic devices. Schools are famous for this practice, with their armies of assistants to this or that, and co-ordinators of everything they can think of. These positions are worse than nothing, because they create needless layers of bureaucracy and thus hinder the people who are actually trying to get something done. Each department head, or other supervisors, should perform duties similar to others in their department. These working supervisors, or lead people, will be better respected by their subordinates because they are actually in the trenches with them. This also serves to eliminate a layer of do-nothing bureaucracy, because these people will be too busy doing their jobs to engage in nonproductive pursuits.

4. The director is the executive officer of the library. It is only he or she who reports directly to the board of trustees. The director also functions as the expert advisor to the board, who are authorized to act only as a policy making body and not as individuals. The director should be the only employee whose sole duties are administering the day to day operations of the library. The head honcho who is swamped with meetings and paperwork can never find the time to function as an effective leader.

Following chain of command is just common sense. Employees don't like to be given criticism and instructions from several different supervisors. This is very confusing, and should be used only if you want your employees to develop an ulcer or have a nervous breakdown.

10. Decentralization: The Key to Empowering Those Who Can Get Things Done

"Here lies a man who knew how to gather around him men who were more clever than himself"
—Andrew Carnegie's epitaph

The problem with the training that librarians receive is that is such training is woefully inadequate when it comes to preparing librarians to direct the activities of major libraries. Library schools offer little or no training in the administration of public libraries. As a result, library school graduates leave school with little knowledge, except how to perform at the most elemental level as either a children's or a reference librarian. They may have some minor knowledge about how to function in a very small library, but they know little about managing larger multi-faceted institutions.

Much of a librarian's practical education in the area of public library service is on-the-job training. Librarians who start their first jobs in very small libraries will learn from those already on the job how to develop and provide public library services. They will usually learn only how to run a small library and will not develop the skills necessary to operate a medium or large size library. Conversely, librarians who begin their careers in big city systems usually learn from their superiors how to become bureaucrats. They don't know how to use the personal touch that is such an important part of small library culture. Thus, many small town librarians aren't equipped to deal with the exigencies of larger libraries, and big city librarians become faceless bureaucrats, bogged down with endless meetings and paperwork.

"If I'm doing what everyone else does then I must be doing something right," seems to be the operative phrase. This is aptly pointed out by the comments of a colleague of mine who once had the temerity to chastise me for not attending the endless round of useless committee meetings that are so happily frequented by most of my colleagues. "Librarianship is a profession of committees," he stated. Such brilliance is difficult to fathom. I guess the logic is that if everyone else is a bureaucrat, then why shouldn't I be one too. It had never crossed his mind that there might be another way.

A comparison with the military should help to clarify my position on this matter. If one is trained to be a squad leader, that leader will have intimate contact with the six to twelve people that he or she will be leading. Assuming that this squad leader is doing the job effectively, certain leadership principles should be employed that will gain the trust and respect of the squad and motivate its members to perform at a high level. The fact that this squad leader may know how to be a good sergeant does not mean that the same person knows how to employ the methods necessary to be a general. Both are leaders. (The assumption is being made here that the squad leader is an effective leader, respected by his or her subordinates.) Both must employ basic leadership skills. The general, however, must employ different methods for achieving goals, not the least of which is knowing how to delegate effectively. The general cannot be personally involved with every decision, as would be the case with the squad leader.

The reverse may be true of a librarian who has only been trained to work in a large city library. She or he will likely learn the ways of the bureaucrat, instead of those of the leader. If military officers spend the majority of their careers on the staffs of generals, without a command of their own, then it is likely that they will develop the skills necessary to negotiate the bureaucratic maze of military politics. These officers, however, may be lacking in the personal leadership skills necessary to motivate and inspire those subordinates closest to them. These are the reasons that so many small town librarians don't know how to run larger institutions and why many big city librarians have been bred to be mere paper pushing bureaucrats who are out of touch with their staffs and the public. Knowing how to do one thing does not necessarily translate to success in the other.

By this time, you're probably asking yourself, "What does this have do with decentralization?" Although I may have embarked on a rather circuitous route, there is a point. Both small town librarians and big city bureaucrat librarians have trouble understanding the concept and value of decentralization, but for very different reasons. Librarians from small libraries, which have few professionals, often as few as one, have learned to perform their duties with little help from others. They are jacks-of-all-trades, doing everything from answering reference questions, to checking out books, and preparing the budget. They haven't had much experience delegating to others, because there aren't that many people to whom they can delegate. When they move up to larger libraries, they create their own bureaucratic stopgap by continuing to have most work move through them. It is not uncommon to find library directors of large or medium sized libraries still ordering library materials, although they have long since been far removed from contact with the library's customers.

This is an especially common phenomenon where library directors started small libraries and were forced to expand their operations because of the population explosion of the 1950s, 1960s, and early 1970s. This is a unique variation of "The Peter Principle" (competent people eventually will be promoted to positions that are above the level of their competency). Many library directors, by virtue of outside factors, had been forced to operate libraries that they were not capable of operating efficiently. Small library methods were still being employed in libraries that were no longer small. The directors hadn't exemplified "The Peter Principle" by being promoted to jobs that were above the level of their competence. The jobs that they already had simply changed to ones that were above the level of their competence.

On the other side, big city bureaucrat librarians don't decentralize because they have been trained to guide everything through layer after layer of bureaucracy until it reaches the top for a decision. Bureaucracy has been developed into a fine art. The functions of the various departments are compartmentalized with each department having little understanding of the needs of the others. If the processing department doesn't process the books fast enough, it's the reference or children's department that suffers, not the processing department. Librarians are saddled with an endless array of committee meetings, topped off with mounds of paperwork and reports that must be passed from one bureaucrat to another until they reach the top. There, a decision will be made, or not be made, by a director who is very far removed from the customers. Bureaucrats do not question this procedure. They are not concerned with what is actually being accomplished. Their importance is, rather, derived from their titles and the other pomp and circumstance of their office.

Many bureaucrats relish being bureaucrats. For them there is little hope. It would be a waste of time and money to try to train these people.

Real leaders will realize the waste inherent in bureaucracy and will strive to eliminate it. Whether in a small library or a large one, they will attempt to change the system, not comply with it. Decentralization will be their main goal. That means empowering the people in contact with the customers with the authority to get things done. It is authority that must be delegated, not just responsibility. A common mistake is to delegate responsibility without the authority necessary to complete the task. This is a surefire way to produce an unhappy, frustrated employee. Delegating authority is difficult for many people because it entails trusting and having confidence in employees, attributes not commonly found in bureaucrats.

Here are some simple ways that decentralization can be accomplished:

1. Whatever administrative structure you're using right now, throw it out and start over from scratch. Don't be hamstrung by a format that may not be the best to accomplish your goals. Ask, "What do we need to accomplish and how can our administrative structure best be designed to accomplish our goals?"

2. Eliminate all unnecessary paperwork. Don't just fill out a form. Ask, "Why am I filling out this form? Is it serving any useful purpose? Is the time and money spent on filling out and circulating this piece of paper justified by the benefit, if any, that could be derived from its use?"

3. Whenever possible, give the *authority* to get the job done to the people on your staff that are in closest contact with the public. The reference department, for example, should have full authority to purchase all materials needed by the public. Materials should never be purchased by staff members who are not in contact with the library's customers. Get rid of your acquisitions department and don't assign anyone the sole task of being an acquisitions librarian. The people who develop the library's collections should be the same people who spend most of their time in direct contact with your customers.

4. Don't compartmentalize your library's departments, *homogenize* them. Library operations are dependent on a variety of personnel in a variety of different job titles. If these functions are compartmentalized, no one is responsible for the end product except the director. This usually leads to conflicts between departments. For example, for the juvenile department to function, a variety of tasks must be accomplished, including shelving, cleaning, and materials processing. These functions, in most libraries, are performed by different departments, and are not under the control of the children's department. In this situation, although the children's department is responsible for providing service to children, it doesn't have the authority to control all the functions necessary to accomplish that goal.

All the various job titles should be homogenized under each major public service department, such as the children's department, the reference department or the circulation department. Each of these departments should be provided with all the personnel and job titles necessary to fully complete the department's mission, including such things as cleaning, processing, and shelving. Each department would be a self-contained unit, responsible for all operations required to perform its mission, including hiring and firing its own staff. Once provided with all the resources necessary to accomplish its mission, each department would be given authority to accomplish that mission and would be held accountable. It is the professional staff who are most affected if materials are not shelved correctly. The professional staff would thus have control over the shelving pages. The lines of authority are very clear. Conflicts of interest and buck passing are eliminated.

This concept, which I have called "modular staffing," has been employed successfully for over fifteen years. It has not only been highly successful in providing rapid, effective service, it has also greatly reduced personnel costs. Unfortunately, like most different ideas, it has met with almost universal skepticism and disdain from the library profession. Although this concept is adaptable to any size library, "It wouldn't work here" is the typical remark made by bureaucratic library directors, who haven't even been willing to give it a try. In order to try a new idea, you must first be willing to admit that the old way of doing something isn't the only way, or might not be as good as you might have thought. How many antiquated methods are in use because people have been unwilling to admit and correct a mistake?

There are an infinite number of variations that will work. Don't be afraid to experiment to find the one that is most suitable to your institution. The key is to create a structure that places the authority to get things done in the hands of the people who are responsible for providing the final product to the customer.

11. Learn to Delegate

"Employees like to be treated well, but they also like to be used well"
—Anonymous

Every management book printed today preaches the merits of effective delegation. You can't be an effective manager unless you know how to delegate, goes the lesson. Like much modern management doctrine, some people pay it lip service, but few really understand and know how to implement what today's management gurus are teaching. Managers tend to fall into three basic categories. The first group is made up of those that learn everything available about leadership, and strive to apply it. Much of what they study they have already figured out for themselves and have been applying for years. That magic little light goes off in their heads which says, "Yeah! I knew that. I just never thought it was such a big deal." Lots of people have been practicing management by wandering around (see Chapter 14) for years and never knew what it was until Tom Peters gave it a name. These people are leaders and will spend their lives fine tuning and honing their leadership skills. Effective delegation is one of the most important of those skills.

The second group of managers are the ones who stopped learning anything as soon as they received their degrees in library science. They learn their jobs much like monkey see-monkey do! They watch what bureaucrats do and themselves become skillful bureaucrats. They continue moving up the ladder and are disdainful of any new information that might challenge what they already know to be true. They already know everything there is to know. They point to all the bad examples of management to show why delegation won't work. Nixon wouldn't have had Watergate and Reagan wouldn't have had Irangate if they hadn't delegated so much. The boss has to always be in control. The boss has to do everything if it is to be done right.

47

I have a colleague who barely lets a week go by without telling me how stupid I am for paying attention to any of this modern management hogwash. She preaches, "Don't trust anyone but yourself. Delegate nothing. Keep the power at the top." My answer is always the same. Libraries that are run by leaders that know how to delegate are like America itself. It is not a perfect system, but we have freedom and through that comes innovation and creativity. Because of that, we are able to create wealth as never before seen. Libraries that are run by bureaucratic managers whose primary interest is to protect their power are much like the Soviet form of government. There is no freedom and, as a result, most innovation and creativity are stifled. Whenever a country with a totalitarian form of government is compared with a democratic counterpart, the differences are glaringly evident. Just look at North Korea as compared to South Korea, or the former East Germany as compared to West Germany. When libraries run by leaders are compared to libraries run by bureaucrats, the results are as clearly evident.

The third group of managers is the group that makes a cursory study of management, think they understand its principles and then proceed to pervert those principles. They constantly quote people like Peter Drucker and Tom Peters and pass around copies of *The One Minute Manager* and *In Search of Excellence* for their staff to read. They go to all the state and national library meetings and make nice chit-chat about how they manage their libraries. Unfortunately, the only thing constructive that these people do is talk. They do not actually have the ability to put what they have learned into practice. It could be because of their own lack of self esteem or some other personal inadequacy. Those are surely some of the reasons for the failure of this group to implement what they have learned. The major reason, however, is the "B" Factor. This group of people have an overpowering desire to wallow in the secure depths of a bureaucracy. They don't have the courage needed to be leaders. They can't admit that to themselves, so they assuage their guilt by telling everyone how well versed they are in the art of management. The "B" Factor has again obscured common sense and allowed these people to believe that they are really leaders instead of bureaucrats. They usually reach great heights in the library profession because they are not only good at fooling themselves, they are good at fooling others too—everyone except the people who work for them, that is!

Many supervisors fail to delegate because they don't really understand what the term means. As a result, this is one of the most misused and misapplied management functions. Lack of delegation leads to jealousy and mistrust. To the people working under you, your refusal to delegate is tantamount to a lack of confidence in them. They will feel that you don't care enough, don't think they are qualified to handle more responsibility, don't like them, or worst of all, that you are looking out only for yourself. The failure to delegate can undermine your whole effectiveness as a leader. An important part of learning how to delegate is to examine the reasons that so many supervisors fail to delegate.

1. It doesn't occur to them. Often supervisors are so caught up in the job they are doing that it just doesn't cross their minds that someone else should be doing it. Nondelegating supervisors are so bogged down with trivia that they never seem to understand what their most important function is—to see that the job gets done by those who are working for them. We are most efficient when each job is performed by the person who is most capable of performing that job. This problem is difficult to overcome, if people have been promoted to supervisory roles when they shouldn't have been. Some people are very good reference librarians. They enjoy being reference librarians. When they are promoted to supervise other reference librarians, they try to do everyone's job because they like doing that better than supervising. Some people should not be supervisors. Don't let "The Peter Principle" run rampant in your library.

2. Supervisors view delegation as losing control. Supervisors who are insecure will be afflicted with this phobia. They fear that they will lose their jobs if subordinates are allowed to function independently. They must always maintain the role of Big Daddy or Big Mommy. They have either not learned how, or are not confident enough to take on the role of coach, teacher and mentor.

3. The supervisor thinks that he or she can do everything best. Being a good supervisor is much like being a good parent. Your job is to teach those under you to eventually function as independent productive adults. We have all seen overly protective parents prevent their children from maturing at a normal rate. Those poor kids are in for a big shock the first time Mom or Dad isn't around to cushion the shocks of the real world. Your subordinates have to learn to function without you. They should not be dependent on you for everything. Supervisors should always be striving to get their people to function as independently as possible. The mark of a great organization is not how well it runs when the boss is there, but how well it runs when the boss isn't there. Delegation teaches subordinates to operate independently.

Unless you plan on living at your library 24 hours a day and doing everyone's job for them, you'd better learn how to delegate.

4. Supervisors don't trust subordinates. This is the biggest drawback to effective delegation. The boss must trust those who are subordinate, and that trust is best shown by delegating responsibilities and the authority to get things done. Not everyone will do the job the same way. There are many degrees of skill and speed possible. Not everything should be done the boss's way only. Trust will inspire people and build confidence and initiative. Employees will assume responsibilities and reach standards of excellence that even they didn't think was possible. The leader, through trust, will build the self-confidence and skill necessary for subordinates to reach those undreamed-of heights. I once heard a library director brag, "I trust no one but myself." That message has been clearly transmitted to her staff through lack of delegation. Do you think that there's a lot of innovation and creativity in that library?

5. Supervisors think that they won't get the credit. Supervisors should get the credit and the blame for everything their subordinates do or fail to do. They should be primarily concerned with facilitating the work of their subordinates. All too often it is the supervisor who makes it more difficult for the employees to get their jobs done. Most times this is due to overly critical supervision and failure to delegate to subordinates the authority to get the job done at the lowest level possible. Peter Drucker says, "85 percent of all problems in the workplace are caused by management." Bureaucrats throw up roadblocks. Leaders are facilitators. Leaders will realize that delegation is the key to productivity and everyone will get the credit in a productive library, including the boss. The leader, however, will always make sure to give subordinates the credit. The leader's credit comes in knowing that the crew has performed well.

6. Supervisors delegate responsibilities, but not authority. Supervisors will load their people down with many responsibilities, provide them with little to no training and poor support, and then will come down on them like a ton of bricks when performance is less than stellar. This is a sure formula for ulcers. Responsibility can never be delegated. The boss is always responsible for failures. It is authority that must be delegated; the authority to get the job done with a maximum of latitude and a minimum of bureaucratic hassles and supervision. That requires large measures of skill, self-confidence, courage, and TRUST on the part of supervisors. Birds of a feather flock together. If you don't have

what it takes, you probably haven't surrounded yourself with people who do.

The ability to delegate is a rare quality. Many people who take pride in their ability to delegate actually do it quite badly. On Monday a supervisor gives a job to a subordinate. The subordinate hasn't been properly trained in how to do the job. He is given inadequate instruction and insufficient support staff to complete the assignment. This employee has been set up with a no-win situation, while the boss thinks he or she has delegated.

On Tuesday the boss is on the employee's back because the job is taking too long or isn't being done exactly the way the boss would have done it. On Wednesday the boss delegates the same job to someone else. On Thursday the boss decides that both of these employees can't cut the mustard, and so does the job him or herself muttering, "If you want to get something done right around here, you've got to do it yourself." This bureaucrat actually thinks he or she's an effective delegator.

Your library must be kept on a straight path which you have set for it. In certain emergency or critical instances, control must be firm and absolute. At most times, however, organizational efforts must be directed towards a common goal, while at the same time allowing individual employees the widest latitudes in reaching that goal. Drive and enthusiasm must be maintained. Employees should not be hamstrung by useless bureaucratic rules and fearful of the bureaucrats who perpetrate those rules, but rather should feel empowered to plunge ahead on bold courses of action. Time invested in learning to delegate is like money in the bank. It is an investment in the future of your library.

Here are some ways to start practicing effective delegation:

1. Pick the right person for the job. This is 90 percent of the battle. This is a talent. Not everyone has it. Have the highest expectations of your people and most of them will rise to meet those expectations. If you've hired the right people in the first place, and then trained and motivated them, you'll probably be pleasantly surprised how easy it is to pick the right person for the right job within the organization. People are pretty adaptable. Don't stifle them with overly restrictive job descriptions. Be flexible and they'll reward your library beyond your wildest dreams.

2. Provide your people with the proper training and tools. I once saw a library director promote a clerk to a supervisory position and then

was very annoyed when this person disappointed the director by being a total failure at this job. The harder she worked, the more confused she got and the angrier her boss got. This woman had never been given any supervisory or decision making responsibilities before she was made a supervisor. She was never sent to a seminar, a training course, or given any on-the-job training concerning the duties and responsibilities that she was being asked to undertake. To top it all off, she was given nearly thirty people to supervise, far too many for any supervisor to handle effectively. She wasn't even taught by example, because this director, like so many of our colleagues, spent much of his time at various "professional" committee meetings and conferences. When the director did show up at the library, he second guessed and browbeat the staff for not doing things exactly as he would have done them. If he had just stayed away altogether, the library would have run much better. The staff were very capable of defining and performing their duties. The director's only effect on them was to dampen creativity and lower morale. This is true of many bureaucratic library directors. If they simply didn't show up for work, the library would operate more efficiently. The taxpayers would be better served if these folks were on permanent sabbatical.

3. Communicate clearly the nature and scope of your delegation. There should be no question as to what the responsibilities of the delegatee are. You should give each employee as much authority and as much freedom as possible in determining how to achieve the stated goals.

4. Make sure that your subordinates understand that being different and even wrong is not fatal. You want to encourage independence. Employees will not be able to make their best contribution if they are paralyzed with fear. The boss's way is not the only way, or even necessarily the best way. The people who are actually doing the job usually have the best understanding and perspective. You'll be pleasantly surprised at how many great ideas your staff comes up with that you didn't. That leads to the next principle of effective delegation.

5. Give credit where credit is due. Sincere appreciation for a job well done, or even a valiant effort, must be shown at every opportunity.

6. Never order anyone to do anything, except in an emergency. Request that your goals be accomplished. Everyone is worthy of respect and courtesy. This will become endemic throughout your library. When it comes to delegating, a little courtesy goes a long way.

7. Never allow reverse delegation. When you assign a task, don't have the employee come back to you with every detail. Teach, train,

cajole, encourage; do almost anything except solve the problem for the employee. By forcing subordinates to understand and accept their responsibilities, you will not only reduce time wasted by duplicated efforts, but will enhance their decision making skills.

8. "The buck stops here." You cannot delegate responsibility. The responsibility lies with the leader, no matter to whom the authority has been delegated.

9. Maintain control. Your job is to supervise what is being done without interfering with the process. People who delegate and then forget about the job are not delegating, they are abdicating. Irangate was a good example of this. Reagan delegated a huge amount of responsibility and freedom of action to his subordinates. He failed to understand what they were doing, and failed to pull in the reins when they overstepped their authority. Think big. Plan carefully. Present thoroughly and follow up, follow up, follow up, follow up.

Most people contribute only a small percentage of their potential because they are denied the feeling of ownership, the feeling of personal power. They are often bound by a bureaucratic management system that stifles initiative and performance. Almost all the power within the library rests with those at the top. Mediocrity will be the best you can hope for if your people feel powerless to achieve. The secret of leadership lies in learning how to unleash the hidden potential of people. It lies in helping workers at all levels within the library to experience a sense of control. Leaders increase their control, power and opportunity through the people who work for them, by enabling those people to achieve a sense of power and success. Focus on giving power to your people instead of acquiring it yourself, and your library will reach heights that were believed impossible.

12. Self-Fulfilling Prophecy

"What is life but a series of inspired follies?
The difficulty is to find them to do. Never lose
a chance: it doesn't come every day. I shall
make a duchess of this draggletailed guttersnipe"
—Professor Higgins

Pygmalion, by George Bernard Shaw, is about the power of the self-fulfilling prophecy. As a leader, people will either rise to meet your expectations of them or will be held back by your lack of expectations of them. Great leaders think that most of their people are superstars, motivate them to excel and then get out of their way and let them do their jobs. Bureaucrats have low trust and expectations of their subordinates, and then attempt to control their actions with negative motivations and restrictive rules and regulations. Following the rules becomes more important than doing good things.

There is a great difference between lawyers and leaders. Lawyers are advocates. They must take the side of their clients. They must engage in legal debates that will persuade a judge or jury that their clients are correct. If a lawyer succeeds in getting a murderer acquitted, then he or she has done a good job. It doesn't matter if the client is innocent or guilty. What matters is that the lawyer has convinced the jury that the client is innocent. Leaders should be concerned with doing good things, not in convincing others that they are doing good things when they really aren't. If you are going to be a leader, then you have to be concerned about how things really are, rather than how they appear to others. You may fool the public and the politicians for a period of time, but you'll never fool the people that look to you for leadership.

What is the effect of the self-fulfilling prophecy on the people we supervise? (1) Certain expectations are formed of people. (2) Those expectations are communicated to others with various subtle behaviors. (3) People tend to respond to these behaviors by adjusting their actions and attitudes to match them. (4) The result is that the original expectation comes true, at least in part. (5) A continuous circle of self-fulfilling prophecies is created.

Forming expectations is natural and unavoidable. Once formed, people's expectations about themselves tend to become self-sustaining. We tend to be most comfortable with people who meet our expectations, whether they be high or low. Low expectations on the part of supervisors lead to lower performance on the part of subordinates and vice versa. Better performance resulting from high expectations tends to make supervisors like those subordinates more. The key, of course, is to have respect and the highest of expectations of the people who work for you. Praise loudly and often and criticize privately and seldom; a simple formula, but one that is too often ignored.

Supervisors are usually not so blatantly clear in communicating low expectations to their staffs. The signals are usually very subtle and difficult to discern. Some things that supervisors do to communicate low expectations are: (1) Locating employees in low prestige office areas. (2) Paying less attention to certain employees or smiling less often at them. (3) Not asking an employee's opinion, or showing disdain if it is given. (4) Praising certain employees less frequently and criticizing them more often than others for the same performance. (5) Requiring less productivity from certain employees.

The list could go on and on. The point is that the self-fulfilling prophecy is a wonderful tool for increasing morale and productivity when it is utilized by creating high expectations. Bureaucrats too often use it to create low expectations, and then wonder why everyone around them is doing so poorly. The result is usually more criticism and an increase in bureaucratic regulations. Remember, as a leader, your only purpose is to make the library run better. If that is not what you are doing then you have no function at all.

13. Are You a Bureaucrat-Manager or a Leader?

*"You cannot antagonize and
persuade at the same time"*
—Anonymous

Here's a short review to help you see how you measure up as a leader:

The b/manager drives people; the leader coaches them.

The b/manager depends on authority; the leader on goodwill.

The b/manager instills fear; the leader inspires enthusiasm.

The b/manager says "I"; the leader says "WE."

The b/manager gets there on time; the leader gets there ahead of time.

The b/manager fixes the blame for a breakdown; the leader fixes the breakdown.

The b/manager knows how it is done; the leader encourages people to find the best way to do it.

The b/manager says "Go"; the leader says "Let's go."

The b/manager sees today; the leader sees tomorrow.

The b/manager commands; the leader asks.

The b/manager never has enough time; the leader makes time for things that count.

The b/manager is concerned with things; the leader is concerned with people.

The b/manager lets the employee know where the manager stands; the leader lets each person know where he or she stand.

The b/manager works hard to produce; the leader works hard to help people produce.

The b/manager takes the credit; the leader gives it.

Many managers give lip service to this type of leadership. They like to quote Tom Peters or other management experts and have much of the trendy management jargon down pat. Being a real leader, however, requires a sincere belief in the value and worth of all workers. Bosses who think that they are the only one with good ideas, will stifle the ideas of their workers simply by never accepting them or by taking credit for the ideas themselves.

Bureaucrat-managers usually base their actions on a management theory called "Theory X." This theory states: (1) People dislike work and will avoid it. (2) Because of the dislike for work, people must be coerced, controlled, directed, or threatened with punishment to get them to produce. (3) People have little ambition, desire primarily security, and will avoid responsibility and, therefore, want to be directed.

Leaders base their actions on a theory of management termed "Theory Y." This theory states: (1) Work is as natural as play or rest. (2) People will exercise self-control in the service of objectives which they understand and are enthusiastic about. (3) Commitment to objectives depends on positive rewards, especially those dealing with self-respect and personal improvement. (4) People want responsibility and will seek it out. (5) In the proper environment, people will exercise a high degree of imagination, ingenuity and creativity in the solution of problems.

The basis for leadership is a deep belief in the nature of people as outlined in "Theory Y." This requires the leader to show trust and confidence in subordinates. The leader will be as Tom Peters says: "Empathetic, not sympathetic. A cheerleader, not a cop. An enthusiast, not a referee. A nurturer, not a devil's advocate. A coach, not a naysayer. A facilitator, not a pronouncer."

Use these simple examples and constantly apply them to real life work situations to help yourself move closer to the goal of becoming a truly effective leader.

14. MBWA

*"To profit from good advice requires
as much wisdom as to give it"*
—**Anonymous**

Several years ago a library was designated as one of the most distinguished public libraries in the country, based on a university research study. The director received a very complimentary letter from a venerable library academic in which he asked the director to explain, in further detail, some of the unique features of the library. One of the things that was mentioned in the director's answer was that this library's administration had practiced MBWA (Management By Wandering Around) long before management consultant Tom Peters had ever identified it as such in his book, *In Search of Excellence*. The library director received in return a letter filled with pleasantries, in which Professor X asked, "By the way, what is MBWA?" Mind you, this gentleman had written a well regarded work on library administration that had been used for many years by library school students and library administrators. It was then that I decided that this book had to be written.

There is quite enough literature on the mechanics of library administration. It was about time something was written about leadership, instead of management. A supposed "expert" on library administration who had never heard of MBWA, was just too much for me to bear. If you are a library director who has spent much time attending library meetings and little or no time studying leadership, then you are equally as guilty as this "expert."

Library directors usually spend a great deal of their time at various committee meetings and library conferences. They spend little time studying the skills of leadership and even less time practicing them in their institutions. Library directors need to spend more time in their libraries practicing MBWA. This means that they have to get off their comfy chairs, and out of their offices. They have to bring themselves to the staff and to the customers, so that they can directly find out what's really happening. The library director who sits in the office all day waiting for people to bring in problems is missing the boat. Most staff members will not run the gauntlet of their fellow employees and knock on the boss's door to discuss a problem.

The library director must constantly wander around the library, informally talking to the staff and the public alike. A relaxed, friendly atmosphere should prevail. This requires a high level of interpersonal skills. If handled incorrectly, MBWA can cause employees to feel that they are being over-supervised, feeling that the boss is always on their backs. If practiced skillfully, MBWA will convey to your employees the feeling that you are concerned about them and their problems. This will not only serve to greatly boost morale, but will provide you with a priceless flow of information about improvements and innovations that can be made. The employee that might be afraid to come to your office would be happy to tell you how to improve the library in the informal atmosphere that might prevail at the morning coffee break.

Wandering around also helps to keep the library director in closer contact with the public. I often wander around our buildings and chat with our customers. Most of the time they think I am just another customer, and so are very happy to offer their true opinions on our service. It is also a good practice to work at different jobs in different departments of the library from time to time. This not only helps to give you a better idea of what the customers are asking for, but provides you with your subordinates' perspective on what each person's job is actually like. These informal procedures are far more effective than any formal surveys that could be undertaken.

MBWA is just another form of leadership in practice. Successful military leaders do not become so by remaining aloof from their troops. They are constantly in contact with their troops, and will lead them into battle, should that be necessary. Military bureaucrats will be serving tea and passing reports at high level staff meetings. They may rise to prominent places in the military bureaucracy, but they will never be successful leaders by my standard. When things are running smoothly, bureaucrats will flourish. When the going gets rough, only true leaders will rise to the top.

I am constantly asked why I refuse to attend the plethora of useless conferences, meetings, and other such nonsense that seems to delight so many of our colleagues. My answer is always the same. "I can't afford the time. I'm too busy running my library. You ought to try it some time." A little leadership will go a long way toward improving any library. As Tom Peters says, "At least if you're out of your office wandering around, you won't be in your office writing a lot of useless memos and otherwise making it more difficult for the people who actually have to get the work done."

15. Library Trustees:
Saints or Sinners?

"The road to hell is paved with good intentions"
—Edmund Burke

Every library has a different governing system. In certain types of
city government, the librarian is a department head and reports to one
individual, usually a city manager or the mayor. I much prefer this type
of political organization, because it is the simplest form and because it
follows the "One Boss Only" rule. The library director only has to
establish a working relationship with one superior. This will greatly increase the speed with which things get done, and will not cause the
library director to be torn in several directions by a variety of bosses
competing for power and, thus, slowly going insane. The library director, in this instance, may have to compete with other municipal department heads for the library's share of the tax pie, but any library director
worth his or her salt should be able to deal with that with aplomb.

Unfortunately, the far more popular form of library governance is
the library director reporting to the board of trustees. Sometimes the
duties of library trustees are only of an advisory nature. They are appointed by the city council or the mayor, and may only have limited
powers, such as recommending the yearly budget. Sometimes they are
self-perpetuating boards, where the sitting trustees themselves vote to
fill any vacancies. In most instances, trustees are elected, and serve as
the policy making body of the library to which the library director
reports. Any of these situations are facts of life that are not going to
change in the foreseeable future. Democracy is a wonderful form of
government. It's just that it has its drawbacks when it comes to running
an efficient business, and an efficient business is what the public library
should be.

However the trustees reach their positions, and whatever the legal extent of their powers, the library director still has to deal with them. Library directors cannot be successful, or even remain in their jobs for that matter, unless they learn to traverse successfully the minefield of trustee relations. Anyone who enters this territory wearing rose colored glasses or heavy boots is doomed to failure. Without the full support, co-operation and encouragement of the trustees, the library director will be no more than a figurehead—an office manager with a fancy title.

There are many scholarly materials that have been written about the duties, responsibilities and powers of library trustees. This is what the unsuspecting library director would study as preparation for his or her position. Some of this pablum goes like this:

Duties of Library Trustees. The chief functions of a library board are to learn what are the appropriate objectives for the library in the community, and to secure funds that will make their attainment possible.

It is their duty and responsibility to:

(1) Determine library policies.

(2) Select and appoint the library director.

(3) Advise in the preparation of the budget, approve it, and work to obtain the necessary funds.

(4) Provide the proper physical plant in which the library can fulfill its mission most efficiently.

(5) Study and support legislation which will be of help to the library.

(6) Encourage public support for the library.

All of that on the surface seems very principled and should be supported by all. Quite the opposite is actually true in many cases, however. Horror stories abound. Here's a tongue in cheek scenario that many of our embattled library directors can surely identify with:

QUALIFICATIONS AND DUTIES OF LIBRARY TRUSTEES
OR
HOW LOCAL CITIZENS CAN "RUN" THE PUBLIC LIBRARY.

Sometimes the library can appear to be a smooth running, efficient operation. Like any institution, there is always room for improvement, but, basically, the operation seems to meet acceptable standards. Staff morale is good and turnover is low. Services are of high quality and wide variety. But don't let that fool you. Those underworked, overpaid civil servants must be doing something wrong.

So here's your chance! Become a library trustee and shake them out of their complacency. After all, we know it takes a public spirited citizen like you to keep these lazy louts from further bilking the public.

Here are some helpful hints on how to go about obtaining this position and performing your vital function.

First of all, don't run for election on your qualifications. The less you have, the better. Don't have experience as a manager, a business person or a professional person, or anything else that might contribute to your worth in the position. There are too many college educated intellectuals running things anyway. If you don't have to be elected, but rather appointed by the mayor or some other politicians, your political connections, not your qualifications, are what count. This may very well be the first step in your quest for higher office.

And secondly, campaign on negative issues. Nit-pick. Magnify every fault. Some good examples are: "Every time I come into the library, the staff is always standing around doing nothing; the staff is overpaid; I never get the books I want in time; taxes are already too high." It doesn't matter. Anything will do. The taxpayers and the politicians will love it. You're a shoo-in.

Congratulations! You've made it. You're a library trustee. Now you're ready for phase two in your quest for truth and justice and to provide your community with better library service.

One. Come to the library often to observe the activities of the staff. Don't just remain in the public areas. Wander through the work areas, too. Try to make staff members feel as uncomfortable and ill at ease as possible. After all, you're a trustee now. Start exercising your authority. Besides, what does the library director know about supervision? They're only a librarian. If they knew what they were doing, the staff wouldn't be doing so little. This is sure to keep staff members on their toes.

Two. Expect the director to be available whenever you call or come to the library. There is never any reason for them to be out of the building, and nothing is more important than catering to your every desire. If they're at a meeting, out sick or on vacation, make remarks like "He's never here" or "What are we paying her for?" Do this in earshot of the public and the staff, whenever possible. Generally show disbelief that the director has the audacity to be at the library any fewer than 24 hours a day, 7 days a week. For your tax money, you expect nothing less than total devotion. This is sure to keep the director from goofing off.

Three. Take credit for all the new ideas that work, and blame the staff for those that don't. This is a sure morale booster. Pretty soon they'll be so afraid to act that they won't even make the most minor decisions without consulting you. That's real control.

Four. Ask your director embarrassing and demeaning questions in front of the public and the staff. Always keep them on the defensive. The humiliation will do them good. Undermining their authority will show who is really the boss.

Five. Question every administrative decision, no matter how minor.

Ask justification for every hiring or firing. Find out why that filing
cabinet was needed, and why it needed a lock—and—ugh—who chose
that color? Remember, no decision, no matter how small, should escape
your purview. After all, you are a trustee.

Six. Agree with every critic of the library. They are the voters in
the next election. After all, everyone knows that angry taxpayers have a
clearer understanding and perspective of the library's operations than
the director and staff. They're only looking out for their self interest.
Besides, if you were to back up the director, he or she might not look
for another job and we all know that frequent staff turnover, especially
at the top, keeps the library from becoming stodgy and complacent.

Seven. Hold surprise board meetings and don't invite the director.
That way you will be sure not to be influenced in any way by expert
advice. The director doesn't have the best interests of the library at
heart, but only wishes to increase the bureaucratic empire. It's much
easier this way. The director won't annoy you by questioning your
benign decisions. Keeping them in the dark should help to further their
encroaching paranoid state.

Eight. Scoff at the accomplishments of the director and staff. When
you are shown charts or graphs demonstrating the library's level of
efficiency, laugh and make remarks like, "Statistics can be made to
show anything," or "Statistics don't lie, but liars can use statistics."
Show them that nothing they do is ever good enough. This will serve to
destroy their motivation and transform them into the lifeless
bureaucrats you knew they were anyway. This attitude will come in extremely handy at salary increase time. You don't have to reward the
staff for their accomplishments, because you have already established
that they haven't made any.

Nine. Reject all your director's requests for adequate staff. There's
too much fat, anyway. No matter the justification to prove otherwise,
always claim the library is overstaffed. Don't forget, statistics can be
made to show anything. Also, when the public complains about poor
service, you can blame it on incompetence, and not on a shortage of
personnel. No matter what, you can't lose.

Ten. Don't base the director's salary on the worth of that person to
the library. If they maintain high staff morale and run an efficient
operation, providing quality services at bargain prices, downplay that.
Forget about their years of experience and educational level. Don't
compare their salary level with other government officials, or private
sector managers with similar responsibilities. Instead, keep salary
discussions on a purely personal level. What you get paid and what you
got for a raise is what's important. You represent the average citizen in
the community and what makes the director think he or she has a right
to do any better than the average citizen?

(*Note—This line of logic is not to be used for those who are themselves highly paid professionals or executives. In those instances, you must point out that there is absolutely no similarity between your level of education and the work you do and that of a library director. How could a lowly librarian ever consider receiving remuneration remotely comparable to yours?)

This constant badgering, second guessing and lack of adequate rewards will serve to blunt the director's initiative and provide you with the self-fulfilling prophecy that will confirm your righteousness. The director will be reduced to the uncreative bureaucrat that you always knew him or her to be. If this practice becomes more widespread it will help to attract even less qualified people into librarianship, and thus can contribute significantly to maintaining the lingering stereotypical image of the librarian as the world's foremost dullard.

This may be a composite of a lot of horror stories, but they do happen and more often than we would like to admit. Here's a few pointers on how to lead a board, instead of being led around by the nose. One of your most important functions is to act as the board's professional advisor. This is your profession. You should not turn it over to untrained politicians. Would doctors or lawyers do that? Boards have their purpose and their place and you must be ever vigilant to see that it complements yours and not conflicts with it.

1. Beware of the self-righteous volunteer. This is the trustee who thinks that you're a second class citizen because you are paid for your job. This type of individual thinks they should be canonized because they have sacrificed themselves, free of charge, for the good of the library. Their motives are always pure and just and above reproach, or at least they think so. First of all, there is no way to equate volunteerism with competence. If you don't believe that, volunteer your services to sit on the board of General Motors, or better yet, tell Harvard Medical School that you want to volunteer to be a brain surgeon on its medical staff. You wouldn't have much chance of getting either position. That is because we all know that education and experience are prerequisites for attainment of those positions. We assume that anyone can be a library trustee, because no qualifications are required. This is an insult and a disservice to the profession.

2. Never assume anyone who serves on a library board is anything more than a politician. Like all politicians, they can range from egomaniacal, self-serving liars, crooks and despots to statesmen and stateswomen deserving our highest respect. Franklin D. Roosevelt and

Richard Nixon were both politicians, although history will no doubt accord quite a different place to each. Many directors make the mistake of assuming that trustees, across the board, are a well-educated, skillful and highly principled lot. Then they are surprised when they are blind-sided by a trustee who acts stupidly or underhandedly.

Try using the reverse Theory X and Theory Y method to avoid this trap. Always treat your staff, from the very outset, as loyal, trustworthy, hardworking individuals. Force them to prove otherwise to you. They usually won't. Always treat board members as conniving two-faced politicians. Also force them to prove otherwise to you. The better ones will pleasantly surprise you, but the bad ones won't easily gain the upper hand. It's a big bad world out there. If you can't garner the support of the majority of your board, you're a dead duck.

3. Always remember that the power of the board is vested in the board as an entity, not in individual trustees. You are the chief executive officer. Executive means to execute—i.e., to do.

I have seen directors function as little more than high priced office managers because they didn't understand this distinction. They go to each board meeting with a laundry list of items that they should have acted upon, but either out of indecision or fear have passed responsibility for to the board. The board often doesn't have time to give proper concern to important policy issues because they're so bogged down with trivia. Meddlesome board members will think this is their job. The better board members will know that there is a real problem here, and that problem is your lack of leadership.

Library directors can have their authority eroded by an overly involved board, but I think the more common case is where the director just gives away the store through failure to act. Board members have no executive authority. They are empowered to attend board meetings, discuss policy issues, and vote on them. This concept has been upheld in both U.S. and Canadian courts. If board members overstep their authority, it's the director's job to educate them concerning their proper roles and the proper division of duties and authority. That takes both knowledge and courage.

4. Be aware that trustees usually are not representative of the community, although they like to think they are. Charlie Robinson, the dynamic and controversial director of the Baltimore County Public Library in Towson, Maryland, said in a September 1, 1989, *Library Journal* article, "Can We Save the Public's Library?"

Boards and commissions . . . particularly boards of cultural institutions . . . are generally drawn from the ranks of the elite. Elite, in this case, may or may not refer to wealth, but certainly to education and some position in the community.

The larger the library, the more elite the board. In the largest libraries wealth and social position are almost prerequisites for gaining a seat on the board. Rarely does a library board represent a cross-section of the community.

This fact is not necessarily horrible, but it severely limits an important function of a trustee, that of being able to see the library from a customer's point of view. For that reason, trustees who rarely or never use the library are seriously deficient.

5. Beware of the professional joiners. Often conflicts occur between certain trustees and the director because the trustees reached their position through community service. This could mean anything ranging from fund raising for the local health clinic, to PTA membership or community activism as part of a civic association. These people did not have executive directors to head their organizations and had to do almost everything themselves. They like to be involved and aren't satisfied limiting their activities to policy matters and leaving the day to day operations to the director and staff. It is a difficult job for the director to wean these people from their activist role. If the director shows skill in this area, these people can be fine trustees; if not, there will be a constant clash over who does what. The professional joiner–community activist has stymied many a promising director's career.

Whatever you start with as a board is what you will have to live with for some time. You must be able to evaluate whether or not the situation is salvageable. If you don't have the skill necessary to win over the majority of the board to your way of thinking, then you don't have what it takes to be a successful library director. Think about doing something else. Our ranks are already overpopulated with spineless wimps.

When there is an opening for a new trustee you should have maneuvered yourself into a position where you can exert considerable influence in the choice of the new person. This doesn't mean that you want a trustee who is in your pocket. It means that you want a trustee who fits certain basic characteristics that will make it more likely that he or she will help, not hinder, the library. Don't ever leave this to chance. One rotten apple can spoil the barrel. Here's some of the characteristics that you may find helpful in your quest for the perfect trustee:

Seek a normal person. What is that? I'm not really sure. Use your best judgment. Try someone who appears to display at least a modicum of common sense. That's a very rare, but rather essential qualification.

Avoid those with severe neurosis, psychosis, overly inflated egos and other obvious brain disorders.

Avoid convicted felons, especially if the conviction was as a direct result of former public service.

Don't be impressed with educational qualifications. Cops, firemen, housewives, and factory workers can be excellent trustees, and lawyers, professors, and doctors can be terrible ones. You're not asking them to practice their professions; just to make reasonable decisions concerning library policy. Beware of anyone who actually seeks the job. They may be self-righteous do-gooders, may be seeking political power, or may be negative, one-issue candidates. With all the potential liability that trustees are exposed to today, you should be suspicious of anyone's motives who actually wants the job. Every time I found qualified candidates, I had to beg them to take the position. I have never had anything but a winner from this group.

Seek a candidate who is an avid library user. This is essential if they are going to fulfill the important role of acting as a resource person from the customer's point of view. I have seen non–library users perform adequately, but I have never seen an outstanding trustee come from the ranks of the nonusers.

With your present and future board members, realize that the care and training of trustees is an ongoing process to which you must remain ever vigilant if you wish to avoid the hangman's noose. Try to use some of the following information as a general guideline in training trustees and evaluating their performance:

Trustee Quiz: answers to be used to assess board service and avoid major foul-ups.

1. What are your personal motives for being a board member? Are you using board membership as a stepping stone to another elective office? Do you have a personal vendetta against someone or something in the library? If your motives are "self" oriented, your actions will ultimately not be in the best interests of the library. This is a very difficult question to answer because many people have the ability to lie to themselves as well as others. They really believe that their motives are pure, even though they may not be.

"What is a good man?
Simply one whose life is useful to the world.
And a bad man is simply one whose life is harmful to others.
There are, however, those who are harmful and yet enjoy a

good reputation, and who manage to profit by a show of
unselfishness.
Those are the worst of all."
[From a conversation between Chang Chao and Hanchen in
the 15th century.]

2. Do you know what your primary duties are? They are to hire
a good director and support him or her. If you can't do that, fire the
director and get one that you can support. After that, listen to the director's recommendations and set policies that will be in the long term best
interests of the library. Then get out of the way and let the director do
the job. Don't get involved in administrative details. Everyone who
wants the board to override the director's decisions and make policy exceptions thinks that their situation is unique. The director, not the
board, is in the best position to implement policy.

3. Are you a good listener? Listening skills are an important part
of a board member's job. When you talk, all you can say is something
you already know—or think you know. When you listen, you might
learn something. Listen to all the available facts. Make sure the problem is clearly understood before you make a decision.

4. Do you know how to handle complaints? Don't get caught in
the middle between the director and the complainant. If you gain a
reputation for accepting a third party role in disputes, you'll be a busy,
but not very helpful trustee.

5. Do you understand that actions and offhand remarks and opinions of your spouse and family members will often be considered as actions of your own? Restraint is a virtue, and spouses must not publicly
criticize library policies or personnel any more than the trustee should.

6. Do you know how to make reasonable and fair decisions? Once
you've listened to the public, make sure to collect all the information
before you try to make a decision. Acquiring all the facts is the best defense against irate patrons who might pressure you to make a rash or pre-
mature decision. Don't stick to a position for the sheer purpose of exert-
ing your influence or saving face. Be flexible and open minded enough to
change your position if the facts and best interests of the library so dictate. Saving face is not more important than saving the library. Be big
enough to eat crow if you have made a hasty decision. Everyone makes
mistakes. You don't belong in your job only if you make too many.

7. Do you know how to deal with personnel matters? Here's some
rules to follow:

    (a.) Don't ask or encourage personnel to be critical of

superiors. Your director and his/her staff aren't going to perform any better if you have a spy on the staff second guessing every decision of the administration.

(b.) Don't ask anyone on the staff to bend the rules. Set a good example by following the policies that you set. If you bring back overdue books, pay the fine. It doesn't impress the clerk at the desk or the other people in line to hear you say, "I'm a trustee. I don't have to pay fines."

(c.) Don't ever ask to have a friend or relative employed. The public library is no place for political patronage jobs. Just think of the awkward position this puts the library supervisory staff in. If your friend turns out to be a lousy employee and has to be disciplined or discharged, you'll find yourself in the middle of a very unpleasant situation that should be none of your business. If the director and supervisory staff are going to maintain good order and discipline, how are they going to do it when there are two classes of employees—those who have friends or relatives on the board who can exert political influence and those who don't. The ones who don't are going to resent your interference, as will the director, and the supervisory staff.

(d.) Never give a direct order to an employee. You have no executive authority. If you do give an illegal order to an employee and he or she unwittingly follows it and causes harm to the library, to self or to others, you might be personally liable for damages.

(e.) Never enter the work areas of the library without permission. This is not conducive to a happy work atmosphere for the staff and creates serious problems concerning safety. Staff areas are for the staff. You have no business there and if you enter there without permission, you might be subject to an action if the staff feels they are being harassed or safety is compromised because of your presence.

8. Learn to recognize and deal with stress, a likely byproduct of your service as a trustee. Stress tends to lower perception, impair thinking, and can contribute to impatience and over-reaction, none of which will enhance your decision making skills.

The basic text that library directors should constantly refer to in matters relating to library politics is *The Prince* by Machiavelli. If you don't understand it and how to apply its principles, get another job where you won't have to deal with people. Try accounting.

> *"Being on the spot, one sees trouble*
> *at its birth and can quickly remedy it"*
> **—Niccolo di Bernardo Machiavelli, 1513**

16. The Dynamics of Dominance

"Good teaching is one-fourth
preparation and three-fourths theatre"
—Gail Godwin

The term dynamics is used here to identify power situations that occur as a result of the interaction of people. In your position of leadership as library director, you will constantly be faced with a variety of situations where you will be called upon to exercise dominance and control. Chapter 17 deals with this subject by showing how the board of trustees and director can maintain such dominance and control when faced with an angry and unruly crowd at a public board meeting. As library director, that is only a small part of the skills you will have to master in this area if you are to be a highly effective leader.

Situations where you will be required to maintain dominance and control include, but are not limited to: (1) Daily interaction with subordinates. (2) Interaction with colleagues and other public officials. (3) Dealing with unhappy customers. (4) Dealing with disgruntled employees. (5) Meetings of the board of trustees.

General Rules

1. Always maintain the presence of a leader, someone in control and confident of your actions. Avoid informal clothing. Read some magazine articles or other materials that deal with power dressing for executives. Maintaining a commanding presence is 50 percent of the battle. If you look like an unkempt country bumpkin, don't be surprised if people tend to treat you like one. The library director should be a respected professional. Dress and act the part.

2. Whenever possible, deal with others on your turf. Whether it be a staff member, customer, or board member, always deal with them where you can be in control of the environment.

3. Never discuss problems relating to individuals with uninvolved

parties observing. Deal with an angry patron alone, face to face. Deal with disgruntled employees in private. If it is an individual problem, deal with the individual alone, eyeball to eyeball, in an environment in which you have total control.

4. Always conduct business in an environment that puts you at your best advantage. This means that you should have several areas of the library that you can utilize to deal with various types of interactions that are suited to the type of persons and problems involved. These must be determined and set up in advance; a small quiet area near the public areas where you can quietly discuss a problem with an angry customer, a place to deal with salespeople, and of course adequate areas to deal with staff members and the board of trustees.

5. The first rule is privacy. Staff members do not like to be embarrassed by hearing criticisms or being chastised in front of others. Unhappy customers most often are more reasonable to deal with privately, one on one. One of the reasons for this is that some people attempt to dominate or control the situation by loudly airing their grievances in public. They are often more interested in the feeling of power that comes with drawing attention to themselves, than they are in actually solving a problem, even though they may not themselves realize this. Private meetings neutralize this aspect of the discussion and give you the edge. Now you are not on the defensive, but rather in a favorable position to "turn on the charm."

6. When dealing with staff members or trustees, you need a large enough office and, ideally, an additional conference room that can be set up in a manner that puts you at best advantage to deal with a variety of situations. No matter how small your library, you must be able to establish such areas. Even an area that is primarily used for other purposes, but can be easily adapted for your use, such as adapting a lunch room to be used a board or conference room, is better than nothing. This is not a minor aspect of your effective functioning as library director. Look upon this as one of the essential tools of your trade. You must have a variety of areas that can be readily adapted and used to suit your purposes.

7. If the situation requires that you maintain dominance, sit behind your desk. It should be a large, impressive desk. Have your adversary sit on the other side of the desk. The chairs on the other side of your desk should be lower than your chair. This arrangement automatically places you in a position of dominance. Don't overdo this by having the chairs in front of your desk so small as to make it obvious

what you are doing. This will be effective if handled subtly. If you want to maintain a dominant, but more friendly, atmosphere have your adversary sit in a chair to the side of your desk.

8. If strong dominance is not required, and you wish a more friendly, relaxed atmosphere to prevail, have a small round conference table ready where matters can be discussed in a configuration that allows no one person to sit in a position of dominance. For this approach I rather prefer a sofa and coffee table arrangement. Place a low coffee table in front of the sofa with comfortable lounge chairs at each arm of the sofa. This is a friendly, relaxed arrangement, while at the same time offering you a variety of seating arrangements that you feel would work to your best advantage. This should serve to calm an otherwise stressful or hostile situation.

Controlling Board Meetings

By far the most important aspect of this subject is the arrangement of the room used for board meetings.

1. Use a multipurpose meeting room for board meetings. Never use a room designated as a board room just for board meetings. This is a waste of valuable space and can give trustees the impression that they have an office at the library. The power of the board is vested in the board as an entity. Trustees have power only as a body at a legally convened meeting. They should not be in the staff areas of the library other than to attend a legally convened meeting or to meet with the director, by appointment. Under no circumstances should trustees feel that they can just drop in on you unannounced when the mood suits them. This should be considered a highly unprofessional insult. A separate board room can encourage over-zealous trustees to use a board room as an office or as an informal meeting area which they feel free to use other than at legally convened board meetings. This is verboten.

A conference room can increase efficiency by providing a private area for your other supervisory personnel. You are not the only one who requires privacy. Such a room can be multifunctional, serving as a meeting area for such purposes as salespeople making presentations, group staff brainstorming sessions, or even a quiet place for your independent auditor to complete a monthly review of your account books.

2. When holding board meetings in this multipurpose conference room, it should be arranged so that the director, board president, and trustees are in a position to maintain maximum control of the audience (and see Chapter 17). The director should be in the most favorable position to control the activities taking place in this area. This is the most important aspect of your job. Without the respect, confidence and support of your board, you will never be an effective director. Everything else that you do relies on your success in this area.

3. Provide sufficient seating for outside observers, usually facing the board table.

4. Board members should be arranged around the table in a semicircular (not fully circular) fashion so that they face each other *and* the audience.

5. The president of the board and the library director should both be in power positions at the head of the table, either both at the same end, or at opposite ends of the table. I have observed situations where the director sits in the audience with the taxpayers or even at another table with the rest of the staff. This obviously sets a tone that places the director in a weakened position. The main function of the president of the board is to conduct the board meeting, but never forget that the director is the chief executive officer of the library and the board's expert advisor, not just another staff member.

6. Have chalk board, slides, videos and any other aids positioned in their proper places and thoroughly checked out. Have spare equipment and parts ready anticipating a breakdown. If you need to refer to a visual aid to make a point, nothing is worse than to have it fail to function. It causes you to break your rhythm and also causes the audience to lose confidence in you.

7. The director, and only the director, reports directly to the board. The director may wish certain staff members to attend a board meeting to act as resource persons. Any staff members who attend board meetings should be there only at the request of the director. They are there to answer questions posed to them by the director. If trustees direct questions to other than the director, they should answer only if asked by the director. This will help to establish clearly that it is the director, and the director only, who is in charge of the staff. Subordinate staff members should be seated at a separate table behind and to the right or left of the director. If this is skillfully and tactfully handled it will subtly serve to enhance the control exerted by the library director.

If improperly done, it will allow board members and staff to undermine the authority of the director.

8. Place name signs in front of all trustees. This has the multipurpose function of identifying them for members of the public, and makes board members feel important. Its most significant function, however, is to allow you to designate where everyone sits, thus allowing you to control the meeting from its very beginning.

9. Never allow your allies to sit next to your adversaries. If necessary, use staff members to sit at the board table to separate certain board members. The advantages of separating political alliances should be obvious. Trustees and the director should be working as closely as possible as a team, not as fractionalized voting blocks, where the director and trustees function more as adversaries than as team members. More power is thus implicitly ceded to the director. If your library board and staff have a history of using confrontation as a means of reaching decisions, this will be extremely difficult to implement. If you have the skill and the determination, however, it can be done, but it may take years. Don't expect overnight miracles.

10. Always use a director's report as part of the meeting. Mail it to the trustees several days before the meeting and include as much information as possible in it; staff appointments, financial reports, program and circulation statistics, and so on. This allows the board to review data prior to the meeting and usually saves a lot of time consuming questions. Flood your trustees with information. The more the better. Trustees don't like surprises. A motion accepting the report of the director has the multifunction of avoiding having to make separate motions on a variety of standard perfunctory matters, such as approval of bills and staff appointments. When it comes to your place on the agenda to present your report, they will all have had an opportunity to review the material prior to the meeting. This will usually produce more meaningful questions as well as keeping questions to a minimum. Also, at this point in the agenda, the spotlight is on you. You can highlight areas of the report that you feel need special emphasis, or can use it as a springboard to introduce new matters for consideration. This is a more informal relaxed method of laying the groundwork for some future discussions on matters that you want to introduce, but not discuss in detail until a later date. It is much better than introducing this material under the more formal "new business" section of the agenda. Again, this device serves to place the focus and control in your corner. Subtle, but very effective.

11. Always have some "fillers" ready for discussion. These are unimportant items that can be brought up as time killers or to get the trustees away from a discussion that appears to be headed in an area where you may not be adequately prepared to win the day.

12. Begin each meeting formally. Set a businesslike tone. Non-controversial items that are likely to find universal agreement should be discussed first. This sets a positive tone and gets them used to saying "yes." Save important items for late on the agenda. Tired and hungry trustees are less likely to filibuster and more likely to cut to the heart of the matter and make a decision. Really controversial items can be discussed at dinner meetings. This is a friendly informal atmosphere that will be to your benefit in helping to swing trustees to your point of view, even if they do not choose to make a final decision on certain matters until a later, more formal, meeting.

13. Never play one board member against the other. Provide all the trustees with the same information at the same time. This will increase the trust they have in you and serve to enhance board harmony.

14. Make sure your board president is a trusted ally and is well versed in parliamentary procedure. He or she has to control the meeting. A weak board president will likely allow meetings to become fruitless debating sessions, where much is said, but little is accomplished.

Your style will determine how much of this advice you can and will utilize. I think you'll find that most politically successful directors would agree with most of it, even if to some, it may seem a little too blunt. It's advice that I developed in over twenty-five years of dealing with trustees. It has always held me in good stead. I believe it can do the same for you.

17. Handling Volatile Board Meetings

"One of the greatest victories you can gain over your adversaries is to beat them at politeness"
—Anonymous

Library boards, like most public bodies, are increasingly coming under hostile attack because of the nature of issues that they must now deal with. Conflict with members of the public is a likely by-product of discussion of controversial matters such as, for example, censorship, or salary negotiations which are going to affect taxpayers' pocketbooks. It goes with the territory, so both you and your board must be prepared for it. Your board must not allow angry taxpayers to negatively affect the responsible stewardship of your library. It is one of the prime responsibilities of the library director to demonstrate strong leadership in this area.

Keep your antennae constantly tuned to the vibrations in the community. The fact that a board policy exists doesn't mean everyone is up to date on its contents or its potential ramifications. When angry taxpayers attend your board meeting, it would be nice to be able to intelligently address their grievances, rather than to be caught with your collective pants down. To avoid unpleasant surprises, you need a good communications system that will alert your board to potential problems so that steps can be taken to understand and resolve potentially volatile situations before controversy erupts. It is important to keep influential members of the community informed of issues so that you can gain their support and draw upon their ability to positively influence public opinion. Problems often become worse than they should have been because the library director has not responded quickly enough to a taxpayer's dissatisfaction, or has failed to do the necessary homework that would have anticipated a problem. You and your staff must investigate potential problems immediately. A quick response and a show of concern on the part of the library director can serve to substantially cool emotions before they reach the boiling point, and the board room.

Your board and you should constantly be trying to develop and update thoughtful policies that deal with issues likely to result in public dispute. It is difficult to arrive at a sound policy after angry taxpayers have put you in the hot seat. You will feel more confident when trustees are guided by policies that are adopted after calm and thoughtful deliberations.

Policies that are developed as a result of input from community members are obviously more likely to meet with widespread support. Board members should constantly be receiving a stream of information that will leave them as prepared as possible to deal with unexpected eventualities. Board members who are well informed and well prepared are better able to use their good offices to calm critics before they hit a flashpoint. Strive to be as forthright as possible. Critics will pounce on you like vultures if they feel that they are getting a snow job.

Despite the best planning, you are still going to experience situations involving angry taxpayers that will be extremely unpleasant. Here's how to stay in control of such situations:

1. Critics can be very vocal and it's easy for the media to focus on unfounded emotional attacks, rather than the facts. Always have documentation of relevant data that can be readily provided to both the public and the media. This will show that you are not attempting to stonewall or hide anything.

2. Angry people generally feed upon each other's anger. They become convinced that everyone agrees with them. Seek out those in the community who hold a different point of view. Encourage them to attend meetings and speak out in a positive manner. Critics who are used to feeling heady after receiving accolades for their remarks will likely have some wind knocked out of their sails when another taxpayer, not a board member, disagrees with them.

3. Always attempt to manipulate the actions of the crowd by controlling the arrangement of the meeting room. Use a room that is large enough to seat everyone, but small enough to avoid a theater-like atmosphere. The more intimate, the more friendly the atmosphere. Allow no one to stand or wander around the room. Establish decorum right at the start. The use of the smallest size room possible lessens the impact of any attempts to present a show of force. Encourage eyeball to eyeball contact, discourage theatrics.

4. Require all speakers to identify themselves by filling out a sign-in

sheet before the meeting. They should be required to state their names and addresses and the nature of their proposed comments. You have every right to make sure that they have a right to be there, because they are, in fact, your constituents. Outside agitators will certainly not help the situation. Anyone trained in riot control knows that it is important to identify the instigators within a group. This is not a riot, but the psychology involved is similar. Anonymity worsens the situation. When people know that you know who they are, they are less likely to make outrageous statements or otherwise behave badly.

5. Explain to all speakers that they may each speak only on the subject they have specified for a predetermined time limit, say three to five minutes. Set that limit and stick to it. Only one spokesperson should be permitted per group. Once the time is up, thank the speaker and move on to the next speaker. This will not only be fairest to everyone, but will prevent one or two grandstanders from hogging the show and turning the meeting into a circus. It also gives you another psychological edge by allowing you to dictate the order of speakers as well as the amount of time each will speak.

6. Only allow comments from a podium at the center of the room. Speakers should face the board with their backs to the audience. This separates speakers from their supporters. The agitator who likes to "work" the crowd or who might shout or insult you is often more subdued when standing alone, not surrounded by supporters. The use of a podium also lets you control the number of speakers speaking at any one time. Never allow comments from anyone other than those authorized to speak at the podium.

7. The board can also affect the mood of the audience by dealing with a few routine matters before anyone from the audience is permitted to speak. You want everyone to see that you are a responsible body, used to conducting the library's business in a professional manner.

8. Your board president should be skilled in maintaining control of a meeting. That is his or her primary function. Comments should be directed to the president and only that person should respond, when appropriate. This is no time to play politics or look divided. Your board must present a united front.

9. Never tolerate abusive behavior of any type. The board president should immediately stop anyone who has gotten out of control. Adjourning the meeting or ejecting agitators must always be options to be considered. Hopefully, you will never have to resort to such drastic measures.

10. Never allow a staff member to be attacked or criticized in any way at a public meeting. If you hope to keep the respect and loyalty of the staff, the board president cannot allow anyone to be publicly vilified, including the library director. You also would open up some serious questions of legal liability for slander or other charges if such attacks were allowed to continue unchecked.

11. Listen carefully to the comments presented. Always maintain a calm, businesslike attitude, even if you or your board members find yourselves under personal attack. Even though they may not be presenting their gripes in a pleasant manner, these people may still be bringing a valid problem to your attention. Always treat everyone courteously and with dignity, no matter how rudely they may be treating you. You are not there for an argument. You are professionals, interested in what your taxpayers have to say.

12. After each speaker has been heard, the board president should explain that the speakers' remarks will be taken into consideration after board members have had time to give them proper thought. The board should then proceed with the rest of the agenda. Allow no further interruptions. Open meetings laws allow observation, not participation, in public library board meetings. You were allowing people to speak because you wanted to hear what they had to say, not because you had to.

13. Once the meeting is over, the board president should adjourn it and everyone should leave, immediately. Board members and staff shouldn't stand around and discuss matters any further. Your success at the meeting could be ruined by some off-handed remarks made after the meeting.

Handling difficult board meetings is often the hardest part of any library director's job, especially one who is saddled with trustees who love to fight. You'd better be able to become a master at these skills or you're more likely to become a political punching bag than a great library director. As Harry Truman said, "If you can't stand the heat, get out of the kitchen."

18. Flexible Working Schedules

"The inclination to administer, to standardize,
to regulate, ... and therefore constrict
personal activity is endemic in so-called private
institutions ... as much as in public ones"
—John Lukacs, Professor of History

The use of flexible working schedules can be a major factor in helping to attract and retain library staff, and to enhance their job satisfaction and performance. Flexible working schedules can cover a wide
variety of library personnel policies, ranging from the flexible scheduling of working hours, to such areas as the compressed workweek,
parental leave programs, and job sharing. This chapter will deal mainly
with flexible working hours, usually referred to as "flexitime,"
"flex/time," or "flextime."

Demographic shifts in the labor force in recent years have caused
employers to explore different approaches to the standard workweek in
an effort to attract and retain employees. Worker interest in flextime is
related directly to increases in the number of two-career families with
young children, as well as the number of single parents and older adults
in the work force.

According to the American Management Association, the use of
flextime has more than doubled over the past twelve years, with 31 percent of surveyed companies across the country using it in 1987. Only 15
percent of the companies surveyed were using it in 1977. Some companies of note using this system are the American Management Association, Anheuser-Busch, Bristol Meyers, the Washington, D.C., Public
Library, Levi Strauss, Frito-Lay, Kelloggs, Monsanto, Prudential Insurance, Scott Paper, and IBM. Many of the companies using flextime
are recognized as trend setters. IBM, for example, has earned the
reputation of a company that stays alert to the needs of its employees.
As a result of changing demographics, IBM expanded its flextime
policy in 1988, and has continued to be a trendsetter in this area.

A number of flextime variations exist, including those which permit employees to (1) preselect their starting time, with alterations only at fixed intervals, (2) change starting times at will, regardless of the interval, (3) vary time for starting and leaving from day to day without time periods set by the employer, and (4) change both the length of the day and the workweek, provided the employee is present during a core period for a set amount of hours daily, weekly or biweekly.

The variations are endless, but basically they all boil down to allowing employees to choose, within guidelines, their own working schedules. The type of flextime and the extent to which it is used will vary according to the design of the job and the needs of the employer.

The advantages of this system in its various guises are obvious. People who like to sleep late can do so without feeling guilty. People who like to start early and beat the traffic don't have to sit around idly waiting for the regular workday to begin. People become job oriented rather than clock oriented. If a batch of work needs to be finished, the worker can put in the extra hours needed to complete the job in the flexible band at the end of the day and have the pleasure of knowing that he or she has that many hours of credit (time in the bank). If a parent has to come to work late one morning because of a problem with a child at school, or wants to leave early to go shopping, it can be accomplished without apology or explanation. Flextime also serves to decrease absenteeism, as it reduces the tendency for employees to return home and call in sick if they are late, to avoid being marked as tardy. It also allows employees to work when they feel most alert and most motivated to complete their job assignments.

Flextime has been shown to increase productivity and job satisfaction, and improve employee morale and motivation. Savings occur mostly because of legitimate consequences. For instance, idle time at the beginning and end of each work day, typically spent on small talk, is diminished, making those times more productive due to the optional nature of starting time. Also, the flexibility given employees each day allows them greater efficiency. This efficiency occurs because employees are given the option to choose whether to begin or complete a certain project even though it is near the usual "quitting time." Not only is the workplace more efficient, but the need for overtime hours is frequently reduced.

Flexible schedules are almost universal in their ability to reduce congestion at office machines that tend to get overloaded at peak hours. Flextime spreads the workload more evenly. This factor alone is often cited as the most common reason for implementing flextime, and additionally, is the source of most productivity increases attributed to flextime.

Although the advantages of flextime are compelling, there are, however, some downsides to its implementation. It is difficult to implement uniformly with all employees, because of the differences in job requirements, and it requires the full support and proper training of the supervisory staff. In America, where punch-in, punch-out mechanisms are considered symbols of management control, resistance from supervisory authority should be anticipated, and sufficient training will be necessary to overcome this factor.

A public library that I studied, implemented flextime in the late 1970s. Its use had been authorized, not because of any convincing documentation advising the director of its merits, but out of pure necessity. There has been a long time shortage of qualified personnel to work in public libraries. Flextime was one of the many actions this director had found it necessary to take to make the best use of the workforce available to him. One of the reasons that he tried using flextime was that he had always felt that he was happier and more productive when he had control over his own work schedule. If he liked it, why shouldn't his employees?

A brief analysis of the make-up of his library's workforce should help to illustrate why flextime is so suitable to the library environment:

Gender: of the workforce is 98 percent female.

Proportion of Full-time to Part-time: approximately 35 full-time employees, 175 part-time; combined average 105 full-time equivalents. This mix is determined primarily by the availability of labor. A large portion of the available workforce cannot work full-time because they have other jobs, are attending college, or have family responsibilities which preclude full-time employment.

Age: ranges from 16 to 70.

Worker Categories: a. to f.

a. Professional librarians, full-time: primarily women who returned to the workforce after raising a family. The prevalent motivation for entering the profession was to earn extra income, usually for their children's college education. Others work for satisfaction and fulfillment. For some, library employment is the primary source of income. The majority of these personnel were recruited from teaching, social work, and other fields and attended library school for the express purpose of working for this library.

b. Professional librarians, part-time: most working for professional satisfaction and development and to earn extra money. Most are employed full-time somewhere else, usually as school or public librarians.

c. Clerical, full-time: very much the same make-up as the full-time librarians—mothers who have returned to the workforce after years as homemakers.

d. Clerical, part-time: the majority of workers in this category are persons who returned to the workforce to find fulfillment and satisfaction after becoming bored with being full-time homemakers. About one third of this category is made up of students from the area colleges who are earning spending or tuition money.

e. Pages, all part-time: this is a labor class position that is comprised primarily of high school students and older workers. For most of the high school students, this is their first job. Most of the older workers are between the ages of 35 and 60 and have accepted this position because they have few marketable skills.

f. Custodial: comprised of two full-time supervisors, one for the day shift and one for the night shift. All other workers are part-time, and are either semiretired or have other full-time jobs.

Continuing with the public library that I studied: flextime is implemented in the following manner, depending on job assignments:

1. Full-time personnel.   A 35 hour workweek arranged according to guidelines determined by the needs of each department. Each employee must consider certain time slots, such as those where they are on public service duty, as core time, or time that cannot be flexible. By allowing employees to work out schedules within their own work groups, the flexibility of the system is greatly increased. Employees are able to trade core time spots with each other, in effect making even the core areas flexible. Employees are paid premium pay for overtime only when management requires them to work overtime. Voluntary overtime is placed in the employee's time bank as straight time and can be utilized at a later date. An employee could voluntarily work a 40 hour workweek one week and a 30 hour workweek the next, or almost any combination adding up to 70 hours biweekly.

Sick, vacation and personal time off is credited to the employee's bank on an hourly, not a daily basis. An employee, for example, who was to leave early one day, in order to attend to a personal matter, would have the option of crediting several hours of personal time off to complete the required 35 hours, or could make up the lost time at a later date, and continue to save the personal time. An employee who has to work a late night on customer service, could trade the night with another employee, or could work a long day and take the time off another day, or take a long break in the middle of the day and return to work for the required evening public service shift. The combinations are virtually endless.

To be successful, this procedure requires the effective training of supervisory staff to gain their understanding and support. The experiences of this library have shown that the system works best when each group is responsible for covering its own work assignments. As long as the needs of the work group are met, virtually any combination of work, sick, vacation, and personal time can be used by the employee to satisfactorily complete each payroll period. Experience has also shown that this works best when time is accounted for in each payroll period. Depending on the circumstances, however, supervisors will occasionally make exceptions and allow employees to carry time in their time bank for longer periods.

There is also no limitation on the amount of hours or days worked per week. Employees usually adhere to a five day workweek, although some like a six day week followed by a four day week, especially when they are required to work weekends.

2. Part-time personnel. Most employees in this category work an average of 17 hours per week. They try to be as flexible as possible in determining starting and ending times, but this is not always possible when most part-time jobs require the majority of work time to be spent in public service. This is especially true of shelving pages, reference librarians, and circulation clerks, whose duties mainly entail working in public service during peak hours.

Although there is much less flexibility in using this system with part-time staff, its positive effects on them have been quite evident. Like the full-time staff, they have the option to trade time slots, and this goes a long way towards relieving the pressure of always having to adhere to the same daily schedule.

When the majority of your workforce consists of personnel who would find it difficult, if not impossible, to work a 9 to 5 job, allowing them flexibility in their work schedules is not only a great morale factor, but, in fact, will allow you to broaden the base of your workforce. Many people happily working today would not be able to do so if it were not for flextime.

Flextime rates high with workers when asked what they liked most about their jobs. The traditional yardsticks for measurement of flextime's effectiveness are readily apparent at this library. They have no shortage of qualified employees, although this is not true for public libraries in general. They boast extremely high morale and productivity is high enough to make private sector employers envious. Costs per unit of service have consistently declined in terms of real dollars. The turnover is virtually nil, especially when it comes to full-time staff. People want to work for this library. They are happy and productive workers, and they cite flextime as a principle factor in their job satisfaction. Although the use of flextime is rare in public libraries, those daring few that have had the foresight to try it have been pleasantly surprised.

Organizations, in the years ahead, must be equipped to make use of the entire available workforce in their communities. This means that innovative work patterns must apply to all individuals who wish to participate in and enjoy the full spectrum of human endeavor without feeling that there is a basic conflict between their professional and personal needs. Based on current widespread interest in various scheduling patterns, the future will undoubtedly bring greater innovation in scheduling work hours of both full and part-time employees. Schedules will be based, not only on the needs of the employer, but also on the capabilities, commitments and needs of the employee.

The vast majority of people entering the workforce in the next ten years will be women, minorities and aliens. Only 15 percent of those entering the workforce during this period will be what is considered the traditional workforce: white, middle-class males. Public libraries have for some time been staffed primarily by women and others who could not be classified as the traditional workforce. Even though that is the case, libraries have not been in the forefront when it comes to implementing flextime. Even though flextime has a demonstrated record of success, it has not been widely adopted by public libraries. "It wouldn't work here" is the typical response echoed by all too many frightened administrators. All they would have to do is take their heads out of the sand and try it, and the B-for-Bureaucrat Factor would be nullified. Flextime should become the norm, rather than the exception, for public libraries.

19. Performance Evaluations

"Rare is the person who can weigh the faults of others without putting his thumb on the scales"
—Byron J. Langenfield

Historically, civil service programs in government at all levels have had elaborate systems for the regular evaluation and reporting of job performance. Public libraries are no exception. Evaluation programs have become a major part of personnel management systems in virtually all types of organizations. A study conducted by the Bureau of National Affairs shows that among survey respondents, 84 percent have regular procedures for evaluating office personnel and 54 percent have procedures for evaluating production employees. Performance reviews are conducted annually for 74 percent of office employees and 58 percent of production groups. Semiannual reviews are made in 25 percent of the office groups and 30 percent of the production groups. Performance reviews are made most frequently during the probationary period or during the first year on the job.

The purported purposes of these performance evaluations are (1) to provide employees with adequate feedback concerning their performance, (2) to serve as a basis for modifying or changing behavior towards more effective working habits and (3) to provide managers with data which they may use to judge future job assignments and compensation.

Performance appraisals are far more widely used as a basis for making compensation decisions and planning individual performance improvement programs. Organizations of fewer than 500 employees make significantly greater use of appraisals in compensation and promotion decisions than do organizations with more than 500 employees. These larger organizations make greater use of appraisals for performance improvement and feedback.

Some of the performance evaluation methods currently in vogue are:

1. *The rating scale method*—This method is not only used most widely, but also is one of the oldest methods for evaluating personnel. Each trait or characteristic to be rated is represented by a line or scale on which the rater indicates the degree to which the individual is believed to possess the trait or characteristic.

2. *Behavioral Anchored Rating Scales (BARS)*—This method consists of a series of five to ten vertical scales; one for each important dimension of job performance anchored by the incidents judged to be critical. The incidents are located along the scale and are assigned points according to the opinions of experts.

3. *Mixed Standard Scales*—This type of rating scale randomly mixes in one scale, items that measure different performance dimensions. In this scale there are descriptions of three degrees of each trait to which the rater must respond. The rater is to indicate whether the ratee is considered better than the description (+), fits the description (0), or is worse than the description (−).

4. *Essay Method*—Unlike the rating scales that provide a high degree of structure for rater evaluations, the essay method requires the evaluator to compose a statement that describes the individual. This method is often combined with one of the other rating methods.

5. *Management By Objective Method*—This method permits managers to measure both activities and results.

6. *Checklist Method*—One of the oldest methods, this consists of having the rater check those statements on a list that are judged to be characteristic of the employee's performance or behavior.

7. *Ranking Method*—A method of evaluation which requires each rater to arrange subordinates in rank order from best to worst.

8. *Forced-Choice Method*—Developed for use in the reorganization of the military establishment after World War II, the forced-choice method requires the rater to indicate by a check mark those statements that best describe the individual being rated. Since several statements, equally favorable or unfavorable appear, the person completing the forced-choice report cannot be certain whether the employee is being given a high or low rating.

9. *Critical-Incident Method*—This technique involves identifying and recording incidents in employee behavior. Critical incidents are facts (not generalizations or opinions). An incident is considered "critical" when it illustrates that the employee has done, or failed to do, something that results in unusual success or unusual failure on some part of the job. Critical incidents are often used in constructing other types of evaluation procedures such as checklists and BARS. Imagine that; a rating method that is used to develop another rating method. Will wonders never cease?

10. *Work Standards Method*—Many organizations set work standards in terms of realistic outputs. This method is supposed to provide an objective basis for evaluating employee performance.

11. *Field-Review Method*—This method has a technician of the personnel department go to the supervisor to obtain information about the work of individual employees. The personnel technician will ask the supervisor detailed questions about each employee's performance and then return to the personnel department to prepare the evaluation reports. The reports are then sent to the supervisor, who revises them, if necessary, and signs them to indicate approval. How's that for a real personal touch?

12. *Assessment Centers*—Like the field-review method, the assessment center provides for personnel other than the immediate supervisor to participate in the evaluation of subordinates. Primarily designed to identify managerial abilities, the assessment center involves participation of individuals from different departments in an organization. The participants are brought together to work on individual or group assignments under the supervision of assessors. The observations of the assessors are combined to get an overall assessment of the participants' qualifications for promotion.

Now that you have a broad overview of some of the basic methods commonly used for performance appraisal, you're probably wondering which one or ones will be best for you to use in your library. The answer is NONE! Performance appraisals are almost unanimously disliked and mistrusted by management and employees alike. Despite this widespread repugnance, personnel specialists expend thousands of hours trying to devise new and ever more intricate evaluation systems. Personnel officers will claim they are needed to improve efficiency, or to evaluate people for promotions, although they almost never accomplish their stated goals. Some of the reasons for their failure are:

1. Managers see little or no direct benefit to be derived from the time and energy spent in the process. (They're right.)

2. Managers dislike face-to-face confrontation. (Unfortunately, confrontation is the usual modus operandi.)

3. Most managers are not sufficiently skilled in the use of performance evaluations. (An understatement.)

4. The level of standards, biases, and subjective judgments that vary from rater to rater seriously damage the validity of any rating system.

5. The judgmental process required for evaluation is in conflict with the helping role that should be a leader's prime objective.

6. Appraisals are usually conducted as a once-a-year activity, and they often resemble a formal legal case in which the supervisor documents the evidence instead of conducting a helping, motivational discussion.

7. Employees don't like to hear negative comments, especially long after the supposed offense has taken place. Even if most of the evaluation is positive, the employee will tend to give greater emphasis to the few negative points. This will likely result in a negative, rather than a positive, impact on performance.

8. Appraisals are often used by supervisors as a form of disciplinary procedure. An employee is punished at appraisal time for a past error. Performance should be dealt with in a timely, personal and diplomatic manner. Formal appraisals are not the best vehicles for that purpose. When disciplinary action is necessary, it should be undertaken in a form apart from the appraisal procedure.

9. Where real disciplinary proceedings are necessary, appraisals can also work against the best interests of the employer. An employee who might be performing unsatisfactorily can point to many years of satisfactory evaluations, even though those evaluations were done by a different rater using different standards. All too often, performance evaluations become an end in themselves, with personnel officers spending countless hours devising schemes and making countless excuses for the inadequacy and outright failure of these systems. "If only we had the funds, the training time, the personnel necessary, we could make this work the way we know it can." You can be assured that the "B" Factor is fully in effect when you hear remarks such as those.

Some would say that the costs of implementing such programs effectively will outweigh any benefits. I would go one step further than that. Such programs are actually counterproductive. They waste valuable hours that could be spent on more productive endeavors and, what is worse they tend to have a negative, rather than a positive effect on employee morale and performance. That is because employee evaluations formalize and bureaucratize what should be a natural, friendly interaction between employer and employee. They are a tacit submission to the ways of the bureaucracy: the tendency to quantify, formalize, and measure every conceivable human endeavor. It is no accident that such evaluations are more heavily relied upon by large firms than small ones. Small firms more often take a personal, team effort approach in dealing with their employees. A family atmosphere is created. Large firms more often tend to treat their employees like so many square pegs to be plugged into so many square holes. Accountants should stay in the counting room. Like lawyers and doctors, they generally tend to make poor leaders. American business has been learning this the hard way. It is no longer as fashionable as it once was to place financial personnel in top management spots. They are gradually being replaced by more people-oriented, customer-oriented, production personnel. General Motors, for one, has learned that lesson the hard way, after losing a large portion of its market share during the 1980s when a numbers-cruncher was at the helm.

Bigger is not better. Small libraries should not give in to the temptation to imitate large ones. The formula for success is to operate like a small library even if you are not small. The leader should take on the role, not of the controller, but of the coach, guiding and motivating team members towards a common goal. This requires daily personal contact and a high level of interpersonal skills.

Operating a successful business or a successful library requires that the leader take on the role of parent-coach. Like good parents, leaders want their followers to mature, and eventually to be able to function as independently as possible. Employees should always know where they stand, because of the daily intercourse between leader and subordinates. This is an ongoing, informal process. It should not be formalized. To do so is to undermine the very process by which the leader motivates and inspires those under his or her tutelage.

An analogy that I find effective in getting this point across to those that I am training to be leaders is as follows: Do you sit down with the members of your family once a year and provide them with a written performance evaluation? Imagine sitting down with your spouse, once a year, saying something like, "Well, honey, you weren't quite up to par when it comes to doing the laundry, and you're too strict with the kids. Although these shortcomings need improvement, I can still rate you high on our family performance scale because of your outstanding activities around the yard." Of course, this is ridiculous. Your family members should know where they stand on a day to day basis, not through a once-a-year evaluation. Shortcomings and disputes should be resolved in a timely and diplomatic manner. Parents are very much like bosses. A lot of people find themselves in both of those positions without the skills necessary to perform adequately.

20. Call Yourself on the Phone

"What isn't tried won't work"
—Claude McDonald

Good telephone service is the hallmark of good customer service. Often the telephone is the only contact that patrons will have with the library. Patrons who call the library are entitled to the same courteous, prompt service that patrons who come to the library in person receive. Unfortunately, they often do not get it. The direction of calls, and the satisfactory answering of questions, is often a difficult task for the library staff. Customers who call the library often don't ask for a specific person. At other times they may call to ask for a specific person, when in actuality any staff member on public service duty at the time could answer the question. Is the question reference? Is it about an unpaid vendor bill? Is it a complaint about something? Is it a staff member's spouse or parent making a personal call? The person answering the telephone must be able to ascertain the real meaning of the call, much like a reference librarian must conduct professional reference interviews to find out what patrons really need, as opposed to what they say they need.

The person who answers the telephone must be an experienced, mature, reliable individual, thoroughly knowledgeable of the library's operation. If this is not the type of person that is placed in this job, there will be misdirected calls, callers will be cut off, callers will be left on hold and forgotten about, callers will be forced to talk to several people until they reach the one able to answer their question. Simple calls, such as directional calls, calls about scheduling of programs, or calls asking about library hours, will be handed from department to department when the switchboard operator could have easily provided the information immediately and callers will be run through several layers of bureaucracy, being asked innumerable questions before being connected to the right party.

These problems should be familiar ones. One way to check on the efficiency of your telephone service is to take the role of the patron and make a variety of unannounced calls. Ask a question of the reference department. How long did it take to get the answer? Were you served promptly and courteously? Ask a simple directional question. Was it answered promptly and accurately? Another good way to check on your telephone service is to call yourself on the telephone. Were you given the third degree? Were you asked a lot of questions before you were connected to the party that you asked for?

Telephone service to the leader must be prompt and efficient, and reflect the lean and mean organization that the leader would want to reflect as a public image. To the bureaucrat, however, telephone service is quite another matter. This is an area where the "B" Factor comes into play quite often. Bureaucrats tend to look at telephone service as one of the trappings of their office. The more questions the caller is asked, and the harder it is to speak to the director or some other important person, the more important that person must be. We've all run into situations like this:

Operator—"To whom do you wish to speak?"

Caller—"I'd like to speak to the director."

Operator—"What is the nature of your business?" or "Who shall I say is calling?"

These are completely unnecessary questions which serve no purpose except to irritate the caller. When I discuss using a simpler telephone procedure with my colleagues they invariably say that it can't be done. They think that they would be getting many misdirected and annoying calls. Of course, the "B" Factor has prevented them from taking the simple steps of analyzing the quantity and type of calls that usually come to their attention and experimenting with a less cumbersome system.

My analysis of the calls directed to me was as follows:

I receive an incredibly small number of phone calls; no more than six per day.

Surprisingly, somewhere around 95 percent of the callers who ask for me by name actually should be directed to me. It is not necessary for someone else to ask the nature of their business, as I can ascertain that myself when I receive the call. Disgruntled taxpayers are not any easier to deal with if they have been shuttled between several lower level staff members before finally being able to lodge a complaint with someone who could act on it.

Of the small percentage of callers who should have been directed to a different department, I can usually find that out within the first minute of the conversation and I can easily transfer them to the right extension.

Members of the public are so used to getting the telephone runaround that they seem constantly amazed when they ask for me, and I am the first one to pick up the phone; no intermediaries, no questions, no delays. Although I have been using this simplified telephone system for many years, and it has met with very favorable public reaction, none of my colleagues have chosen even to try it. The "B" Factor in action again!

If you want to improve your public image regarding phone courtesy, try the following:

1. Choose only well trained, mature personnel to answer initial incoming telephone calls. This should not be a fill-in job manned by the least experienced personnel.

2. Set the standards, and continually train telephone staff and monitor their performance. Don't wait for complaints. Pretend to be a customer and call the library for a variety of reasons on a regular basis.

3. Take all your calls directly and have your staff do the same. This may make you feel less important, but it will greatly enhance your public image.

4. If you are not in, have messages taken by the switchboard operator, not your secretary. This only causes the caller to be turned over to another party. The message could just as easily be taken by the operator with less inconvenience to the public. Better yet, don't have a secretary at all. That's another expendable position that bureaucrats think they cannot live without (see Chapter 21).

5. Make all your own calls. Never have another staff member make a call for you and then cause the party on the other end of the line to wait until you get on the phone. This is a particularly onerous practice of stuffed-shirt bureaucrats, and it's just plain rude.

The object is to direct the caller to the proper party or take a message with the least amount of time and the fewest amount of library personnel involved.

21. Do You Really Need a Secretary?

"Those who are most impressed by the perks of their office usually are least deserving of them"
—Anonymous

One of the favorite trappings of the bureaucrat is the secretary. This is the same bureaucrat-director who cannot possibly conceive of making and answering his or her own phone calls. In libraries of all sizes the director invariably employs the services of a personal secretary. In the business world, the executive secretary is the universal perk for administrative personnel. The VIPs often have more than one. Depending on their importance, some may even have executive assistants, who constantly hover around their bosses, eagerly waiting to do their bidding. The library director, being the top dog, the logic goes, must therefore have a secretary. In some of the larger libraries, private business may be emulated further and the director may have a whole administrative staff, including secretaries and assistants to the director and other administrative assistant types. What is truly amazing is that even in the smallest of libraries, the director usually has a secretary. This is the "B" Factor in action again. No one has bothered to employ common sense and ask what the secretaries really do. Could their duties be transferred to others? Are they necessary at all? It is just assumed that directors have secretaries, because their predecessors had secretaries and everyone they can think of has a secretary. This is again the result of making a bureaucratic decision based on what inflates the importance of the bureaucrat, rather than on what makes the library operate more efficiently and provide better service to the public.

This, of course, all relates back to the library's basic organizational structure and staffing. It is set up a certain way primarily because it was always set up that way. There is no change, no searching for new and better ways to do things. Although I am the director of a library that circulates nearly a million items per year, and have a budget of approximately

$6 million, nearly $1 million of which is spent on library materials, I have happily operated without the services of a secretary for many years. Yet, not one of my colleagues is even willing to give it a try. Library directors running libraries one tenth the size of mine simply tell me that I'm wrong. "It can't be done," they say. That is an amazingly illogical statement in light of the fact that it is being done. It's mind boggling! The "B" Factor again stifling change and productivity.

Much as I did with phone service, I took a close look at what my secretary actually did, back when I had one.

1. She took and screened my incoming phone calls. The calls I received per day usually numbered fewer than three. Six was usually the maximum number of calls that I received per day. Most people who asked for me actually should have gotten me, so screening the calls only served to annoy the callers.

2. She kept my appointment book. This caused problems, because if I was speaking to someone on the phone and attempting to make an appointment, I had to transfer the call to her because she had the appointment book. I tried maintaining two appointment books, but that was a total fiasco. Once in a while I would attend a management training seminar, but for the most part, my work time is spent in one of our buildings, where I practice MBWA. Since I had almost no appointments, I certainly didn't need an appointments secretary.

3. She made travel arrangements for me. When it was necessary for me to travel to attend a seminar or visit another library, it was easy enough for me to make my own arrangements. It also saved time and was less confusing. The President of the United States may need a travel secretary, but the majority of library directors certainly do not.

4. She sorted my mail. Of all the mail that was addressed to me, 99 percent was junk mail, or bills, most of which had to be directed to other departments. The actual amount of mail that I needed to view each day was under five pieces. After mail was sorted and sent to the various departments by someone other than the secretary, the secretary was reduced to opening the few pieces of mail that were left for me. I soon discovered that I had the necessary skills to operate an electric letter opener, although a manual one would have done nicely.

5. She filed my incoming and outgoing correspondence. Incoming correspondence that required filing amounted to approximately two pieces a day. Outgoing correspondence was limited to about one piece per week. I speak to people personally, whenever possible, thus avoiding much time-consuming and costly paperwork.

6. She typed my outgoing correspondence. As I have already stated, this amounted to almost nothing, violating the age old adage that good bureaucrats are known by the amount of paperwork that they can generate.

7. She worked as a jack-of-all-trades handling a variety of jobs that fell in the cracks. This was mostly done as a matter of necessity in an attempt to fill up her day. These could involve typing personnel folders, typing orders, typing reports, or a variety of other tasks that could have been done by others.

In order to work without a secretary, you must first be willing to try not being a bureaucrat. It is very nice to have your own personal handservant. Your secretary probably. even makes you coffee in the morning. That may be very convenient and may make you feel very important, but does it really make the library run better? If you're a bureaucrat, you couldn't live without a secretary. If you're a leader, you wouldn't want one. You can find another more productive function for anyone talented enough to function as a personal secretary.

For those of you who can set aside your egos for a moment, here's a few ways that you could operate without a secretary and increase your library's efficiency:

1. Take all your own calls directly. Try using an answering machine. I have done so quite successfully. The message could say something like, "Hello, this is the library director. I don't have a secretary, so this machine takes all my calls. After the tone, please leave your name, number and any message. Thank you." The advantages to this are numerous. The taxpayers love it. It tells them right off the bat that you have a lean staff. The messages left are usually clear and understandable, unlike most of the written ones that are taken by the operator. You can hear the caller so you have the option of picking up the call, or if you are in the midst of another activity and don't want to be interrupted, you can let the machine take the message and return all your calls at a later time. This is a recommended procedure, even if someone other than the machine takes your messages.

2. Put a computer in your office and learn to use it. Most messages to staff can be sent through electronic office mail if you can't deliver them personally. For the few memos and pieces of correspondence that you should be creating, it is far easier to type it on a word processing program and print it yourself, than to handwrite or dictate your correspondence. These machines even check your spelling.

3. Maintain a simple filing system and file yourself the few pieces of correspondence that you may wish to keep.

4. Keep your own appointment book. I would advise using a computer program for this, or you could try using one of the new pocket size electronic notebooks. I have one that fits in my pocket in which I keep my entire rolodex file, a schedule of my activities, and any reminder memos that I might choose to leave myself. This is far superior to the paper rolodex, calendars and notepads, as it is actually a tiny computer that can randomly access the information you desire. If you want to remember when your meeting with the superintendent of schools is, all you have to do is type in any applicable reference, such as the word "super," and the information will appear on the screen. The same goes for phone numbers and memos.

5. Many of the other jack-of-all-trades activities normally handled by a secretary should be transferred to other departments. This will be especially easy if you have adopted a decentralized system of modular staffing, where each department is not compartmentalized. Under modular staffing each department is totally self-contained and work such as processing purchase orders, checking in supplies, processing new employees, and a variety of other tasks are handled within each self-contained department. There are no jobs that "fall in the cracks."

Scrutinize every position in the library in the same manner to see if it should be modified or eliminated. This should be an ongoing process. Bureaucracy tends to perpetuate itself. You have to be ever vigilant to prevent that type of stagnation.

If you're a bureaucrat, you love the ego gratification that goes with having your own personal secretary, as well as lots of other useless positions with fancy titles. In a large library, you may have even created the cousin of the personal secretary, the infamous position of "Assistant to the Director for Something." If the array of meetings that you attend and the amount of paperwork that you generate has you convinced that I'm crazy, and that you couldn't possibly function efficiently without a secretary, then you'll probably go right on using one. Real leaders, however, will be champing at the bit, waiting to give this a try. To them, productivity, not ego gratification, is their driving force.

22. Laws You Should Know

*"Be curious always! For knowledge will
not acquire you; you must acquire it "*
—Sudie Back

This is a brief overview of certain federal statutes and regulations that cover a variety of employment actions. The focus of this chapter is in the area of discharge and discipline, because that is where most employment problems arise. Library directors should also be familiar with various state laws which will affect their libraries, especially those concerning "wrongful discharge."

National Labor Relations Act

Library directors may tend to think of the NLRA as a statute that deals only with unionism. This is not so. Your supervisors should be aware that any time two or more employees are acting together to change or affect their wages or conditions of employment, or where one employee is acting as spokesperson for a group, those employees may be acting in a manner that is protected by the NLRA.

Normally, however, it is during union organizing activities that the NLRA limits the activities of management. The union activities or sympathies of employees cannot influence any part of a management decision about the employee's job, especially those actions relating to promotions, layoffs, discipline or work assignments. Only union activities which interfere with work can be the subject of discipline, that discipline being the result of the disruption of work, not the union activity. Consistency and job-relatedness are the keys to lawful disciplinary actions. Employees must be treated in a manner that is consistent with the treatment of other employees in like situations.

Usually the training of supervisors in this area is lax or nonexistent, unless a problem arises. All supervisors should be trained in the proper handling of union activities under NLRA. When a library director

99

learns of union organizing activities, the retraining of supervisors must immediately be undertaken to assure that illegal activities are avoided, some of the most common violations being (1) promises to employees of benefits or special considerations to persuade them from unionizing, (2) questioning employees about their union activities, (3) spying on employee union activities and (4) threatening employees engaged in union activities with reprisals.

The NLRA is enforced by the National Labor Relations Board. The process is that any party, including the employer, may file a charge with the Regional Office of the Board. A complaint will be issued if the Regional Board finds reasonable cause to believe there has been a violation. If the matter is not settled upon the issuance of a complaint, there is a hearing before an Administrative Law Judge. Decisions may be appealed to the National Labor Relations Board and the United States Court of Appeals.

There are no fines, imprisonment, or punitive damages under the NLRA. Remedies involve returning employees to the same place they would have been had there been no discipline.

Federal Labor Standards Act of 1938

This act, commonly known as the "Wage and Hour Law," assures employees engaged in interstate commerce a minimum hourly wage, and pay at time and one-half for hours worked in excess of 40 hours in any one workweek. Certain categories of employees may be exempt from the overtime provisions of the law, so it is important to review the specific criteria concerning who is actually covered. Many library directors mistakenly think that their libraries are exempt from this law, because of the provision concerning interstate commerce and, because, in some cases, state law appears to take precedence. Consult with the Labor Department and your attorney concerning this matter. You may be surprised to find that you are covered. For example, in New York State, the provisions of this law for libraries and other municipal employers supersede those of the state wage and hour laws.

The Act is enforced by the Department of Labor, but employees may file court actions without going to the Department of Labor. An employer may not discipline or discharge an employee because that employee filed a complaint, or filed a legal action to protect his or her rights. Willful violations are punishable by a fine of not more than $100,000 and, in some cases, liquidated damages of double the amount due. A second offense is punishable by imprisonment of not more than six months, as well as a fine. Employees who successfully file actions are entitled to recover attorney's fees. The statute of limitations is two years, except for willful violations, which extend it to three years.

Consolidated Omnibus Budget Reconciliation Act of 1985 (COBRA)

Employers of 20 or more employees are required to offer employees and their dependents certain health insurance continuation rights if the employee is terminated, laid off, or has work hours reduced so that he or she no longer meets the eligibility requirements for health insurance coverage. The employee can choose to continue health care for self and dependents for 18 months at the employer's group rate, plus a 2 percent charge for administrative costs. There are certain instances where dependents can qualify for up to 36 months of coverage. Only employees who are terminated for "gross misconduct" (behavior that is criminal) can be denied health insurance continuation rights.

Additional information about specific COBRA notification and documentation requirements are best obtained from the insurance carrier that handles the health insurance for your library.

Title VII of the Civil Rights Act of 1964

This statute prohibits employment discrimination based on race, color, sex, religion, or national origin. It covers all employers with 15 or more employees. If your library has fewer than 15 employees, they are likely covered by state statutes that are similar to Title VII. This Act covers all areas of employment including hiring, discharge, classification, pay practices and promotion. It is unlawful to deal with any employee in any special or different way in any aspect of employment because of that employee's race, color, religion or national origin. If employment actions are motivated by any one of these factors, the action will be a violation of the law. The most common situations involving Title VII relate to discipline. Problems occur when disciplinary action against a minority or a woman may be proper, but cannot be upheld because similar actions by a Caucasian or a male did not result in disciplinary action. A second problem area is when discipline cannot be shown to be job related. Disciplinary action must be uniformly applied, and must be job related, or your library will be in violation. Proper documentation of all disciplinary actions is essential.

The law also states that if an action of management has a

"disparate impact" upon a person in one of the protected groups, then, unless there is a clear justification for the action, it will violate Title VII. This means that your library can be in violation even if you did not intend to discriminate. This Act does not mean that minority employees and women are entitled to any special consideration. The only two categories of employees who are entitled to special consideration are handicapped employees and employees whose religious beliefs limit some job activity.

Enforcement of this Act is handled by the Equal Employment Opportunity Commission (EEOC). Charges must be filed with the EEOC before taking court action. In states that have their own equal opportunity law, the charge must first be processed by the state or local agency. In conducting its investigation of a complaint, the EEOC has broad powers, including the right to reasonable access to records and documents, and the right to subpoena such records as well as witnesses. The EEOC may also expand the charge to cover individuals not named in the original charge, or may process the charge on a "class action" basis, so that it covers all employees who have been adversely affected by the alleged discriminatory practice.

At the conclusion of the investigation, the EEOC will issue a determination letter on whether or not "reasonable cause" exists to believe that an unlawful act has occurred. If reasonable cause is found, the EEOC has the right to bring a suit in federal court on behalf of the employee who filed the original charge. More often, it will issue a right-to-sue letter permitting the employee to sue on his or her own behalf. The right-to-sue letter is issued in all cases, including those where reasonable cause has not been found. The employee who intends to sue must do so within 90 days of receipt of the right-to-sue letter.

Remedies that may be court-imposed include reinstatement, back pay, front pay (compensatory and punitive damages), and an order to cease the discriminatory practices. In addition, employees who win Title VII lawsuits are entitled to recover attorney's fees and costs from the library.

Discrimination suits are expensive to defend. Well documented personnel files may persuade a potential plaintiff not to pursue a lawsuit. The best protection for your library, however, is simply good leadership. Not only does the law require you to treat all employees equally, it is the right way for you and your supervisory staff to do your jobs. Making employment decisions on any factors that are not job-related is poor leadership. Productivity and morale will not only falter, but you and your supervisors will lose the respect of those you lead.

EEOC Sexual Harassment Guidelines

The Equal Employment Opportunity Commission issued guidelines in 1980 which define sexual harassment in the workplace. The guidelines have been followed by the courts, and their effect is to expand the obligations of the employer in preventing sexual harassment, and to impose liability upon the employer for the conduct of supervisors, other employees and third persons.

Sexual harassment includes unwelcome sexual advances, requests for sexual favors, and other verbal or physical conduct of a sexual nature. The guidelines state that such conduct violates Title VII of the Civil Rights Act of 1964 when (1) submission to such conduct is made a term or condition of an individual's employment, (2) submission to or rejection of such conduct is used as the basis for employment decisions affecting an individual, or (3) such conduct has the purpose or effect of unreasonably interfering with an individual's work performance, or creating an intimidating, hostile or offensive work atmosphere.

These definitions are intentionally broad so as to permit the EEOC to make a determination on a case-by-case basis, taking into account the record as a whole and the totality of the circumstances, including the nature of the sexual advances, and the context in which the alleged incidents occurred. The absence of clear definition, unfortunately, presents problems concerning effective detection and enforcement. Until this area becomes more clarified, libraries should develop and follow simple procedural steps for responding to sexual harassment complaints. Libraries would be wise to take certain preventive actions, which might include raising the subject of sexual harassment with the workforce and expressing the administration's strong disapproval, developing appropriate sanctions and penalties, advising employees of their right to raise, and telling them how to raise, sexual harassment claims under Title VII, and developing and utilizing methods to sensitize employees and supervisors.

Following a planned program of response will greatly reduce your library's exposure to liability for Title VII violations based on sexual harassment. Some suggested actions are:

1. Adopt and publicize to all employees a written policy statement which prohibits sexual harassment in the library.

2. Adopt an in-house complaint resolution procedure for processing sexual harassment claims, and publicize its availability. In unionized

environments, the union grievance procedure can be an appropriate vehicle for processing sexual harassment claims, although some feel that it is not, and prefer the use of an independent procedure.

3. Promptly and thoroughly investigate sexual harassment claims. This will establish the affirmative stance required by the guidelines, and will help to minimize legal exposure under the "totality of circumstances" standard set forth in the guidelines.

4. Make sure your supervisors understand the policy, and how to implement it.

5. Review the guidelines with your attorney. Consult your attorney also in developing your library's policy prohibiting sexual harassment, as well as developing a complaint resolution procedure and a policy statement on sexual harassment.

6. Provide continual training to all employees regarding sexual harassment in the library. A vigorous and positive program will greatly reduce your library's exposure to potential liability.

Pregnancy Discrimination Act of 1978

This act, which is a part of Title VII, states that women affected by pregnancy, childbirth, or related medical conditions must be treated the same for all employment related purposes as other persons not so affected, but similar in their ability or inability to work. It is unlawful to discipline, discharge, or require an employee to take a leave of absence simply because she is pregnant. The same policies must be applied to pregnant employees as would be applied to other employees with temporary disabilities. Pregnant women need not be treated better, but must not be treated worse than other employees with temporary medical disabilities.

Pregnant employees are not entitled to have their jobs held for them for a certain period of time during maternity leave, unless that is the policy for all employees with temporary disabilities. However, if an employee's performance is impaired by her pregnancy, the library can require her to begin her medical leave at the point she can no longer perform all of her duties. If light duty work is offered to her as an option, it must also be offered to other temporarily disabled employees. At this writing, movements are under way in Congress to provide mandatory reinstatement for pregnant employees. Enforcement of this act is through the EEOC, and the same procedures and remedies that apply to other Title VII cases apply in pregnancy discrimination cases.

Age Discrimination in Employment Act

The ADEA bans discrimination against employees and job applicants who are over 40 years of age. It also prohibits mandatory retirement, except for a limited category of highly paid executives. This law only covers employers with 20 or more employees, however, all states have similar laws that usually cover all but the smallest employers.

The purpose of the law is to eliminate discrimination in employment based on the fact that certain employees are aging. If an employee is no longer able to meet uniformly applied work standards, disciplinary action is lawful. The law, therefore, does not regulate job-related discipline. Poor performance is poor performance. It cannot be blamed on age. Supervisors must also be cautioned to avoid making off-handed remarks about an employee's age.

The EEOC is responsible for enforcement of this act. Suits to enforce the law may be brought either by the individual employee or by the government, and may result in back pay and reinstatement. A library's willful violation could result in additional damages, in the amount equal to back pay, a fine of not more than $10,000 and imprisonment for up to six months.

Immigration Reform and Control Act of 1986

This Act requires all employers to verify the employment eligibility and identity of all employees hired after November 6, 1986. Verification for employees hired between November 7, 1986, and May 31, 1987, should have been completed no later than September 1, 1987. For all persons hired after June 1, 1987, employment eligibility and identity must be verified, and INS Form I-9 completed, within three days of the time that an individual accepts an offer of employment, or within three days of the time that employment actually commences.

Consult your attorney and the Immigration and Naturalization Service of the U.S. Department of Justice for advice as to which documents are acceptable as evidence of both identity and employment eligibility. Libraries that fail to check the appropriate documents, and maintain I-9 forms, are subject to both criminal and civil penalties. The criminal penalties include a fine of up to $3,000 for each unauthorized alien employed, and or imprisonment for up to six months. The civil penalty is a fine of not less than $100 nor more than $1000 for each individual who was employed without the required documentation verification.

Occupational Safety and Health Act of 1970

The OSHA requires an employer to provide each employee with the kind of employment, and with a place of employment, that is free from recognized hazards that could cause death or serious physical harm to the employee. An employer may not discipline or discharge an employee because the employee has filed a complaint, testified, or exercised any other rights afforded by this Act.

This Act is enforced by the Department of Labor, which also sets safety and health standards, which must be observed. Upon receipt of a complaint by an employee alleging discrimination, the Department of Labor will file suit in U.S. District Court if it feels that the Act has been violated. The Court may issue an injunction to correct the violation, and order all appropriate relief to the employee, including reinstatement with back pay.

Besides these federal laws, library directors should be thoroughly familiar with various similar state statutes that affect their libraries. This chapter does not constitute legal advice. It is merely a brief overview of some of the laws with which you should be familiar. Laws differ from state to state, and are constantly changing. Much of what is written here will be out of date by the time you read it. You need to be familiar with the law, but should consult legal counsel regularly on such matters, for the most accurate, up to date advice.

23. Collective Bargaining: Comparisons of the Public and Private Sectors

"No matter how right you are, no matter how wrong the other fellow is, no matter how much evidence you have to prove it, you will never get him to agree with you by arguing him down"
—**Anonymous**

If your library is unionized, your dealings with your staff will be much more complicated and much less flexible than they would be if your library was nonunion. Many of the practical actions that you can take that have been described in this book will be much more difficult to implement if your staff is organized. Without a union, you could merely implement a flextime schedule. With a union, that would be a subject for collective bargaining in the next contract. The ideal situation is not to have a union, and, if you are a good leader, there would be no reason for your staff to unionize. People only organize to bargain collectively if they feel they have been, in some way, treated unfairly. If you have been faced with a union organizing campaign, you probably need to read this book. If you haven't, you may have a library that is too small to organize, live in a state where it is illegal for public employees to organize, are merely lucky, or you may be a great leader. Leaders are primarily concerned with the interests of their subordinates, not just their superiors. If that is not the case, then the all too usual system of confrontational management will prevail, where the director will be an advocate for the board of trustees or the mayor, and an adversary to the staff. Whatever the case, it is important for directors of nonunionized, as well as unionized, libraries to have a basic understanding of the collective bargaining process.

Today, one quarter of all organized employees are in the public sector. Almost one-half of state and local full-time employees belong to unions or associations which bargain for them. More than half of all federal employees are covered by collective bargaining agreements. Clues to the understanding of this widespread public sector labor relations activity can be found in the development of private sector unionism in the United States. The private sector, through a variety of legislative acts, operates within a labor relations framework that is basically uniform throughout the nation. Some of the legislation that has developed the framework for private sector collective bargaining are the Railway Labor Act, the Norris-LaGuardia Act, the National Labor Relations Act, and the Landrum-Griffin Act. The uniform national coverage afforded workers by these pieces of legislation is not enjoyed by public sector employees, although much state and federal public sector legislation has been modeled after the private sector. A wide variety of state and federal legislation affects public workers in very different ways, depending on the makeup of the political milieu under which they operate.

Before widespread unionism, public employees enjoyed many advantages over their private sector counterparts. Civil service rules protected the due process rights of many public employees, while their private counterparts could be disciplined or discharged at will. While public employees often earned less than their private sector counterparts, they often received health, welfare and retirement benefits that exceeded those offered in the private sector. For many years, prior to legislation permitting public employee bargaining, the doctrine of sovereignty dominated the scene. The sovereignty doctrine held that the state as sovereign had the right to determine the wages, hours, and working conditions of its employees. This was not only a right, but a duty and was considered to be nondelegable.

Changing political attitudes have greatly changed the sovereignty doctrine, the degree of change depending on the political jurisdiction, and the laws thereof. Collective bargaining in the public sector differs most greatly from its counterpart activity in private industry because of variations in the underlying power relations contexts. As public employee unions increased and became more sophisticated, elected officials found themselves increasingly pitted against formidable opponents. Elected or appointed government officials had neither the time nor the expertise to effectively act as a counterbalance to union activity. The sovereignty doctrine, out of necessity, continued to erode, until today much public sector negotiations are carried out by third party professionals for both management and labor. Public sector collective bargaining resembles the private sector, however, in the range of technology on which it draws. For example, a government machine shop uses the same technology as a privately owned machine shop, and employs workers with the same skills, but market and power relations differ. It is these market and power relations differences that markedly set off the public from the private sector. Librarians need similar education and skills whether they work for school, public, academic, or private sector libraries. The motivations used to attract and retain these librarians in these various types of libraries are also markedly different. The private sector, more than the public sector, understands that time is money and information is power and, thus, is more willing to offer competitive wages to attract and retain the best librarians, because that will translate into better competitiveness and higher profits. If a public library is unable to attract and retain the best personnel, profits do not decline and the library does not go out of business. Service will be poor, and the taxpayers will not get good value for their money. Since the public library is a government monopoly, taxpaying customers usually cannot take their business elsewhere. Although it is hard to draw a sharp line between economic and political power, political influence and sanctions tend to dominate the public sector and economic forces, the private. Public sector participants in the volatile activities of labor-management relations feel the constraints of political forces more directly than their private sector counterparts, who operate in a comparatively simpler and more stable institutional setting.

Most organized professionals are now found in the public sector notably in such professions as teaching, nursing and librarianship. Through education and training, professionals acquire expert power; by social convention and sometimes licensure they acquire, to varying degrees, authority over their occupations and their work lives. This causes an inherent conflict between professional and bureaucratic authority. Elected officials and bureaucrats believe that their positions entitle them alone to make policy decisions. In contrast, professionals believe their knowledge better qualifies them to make decisions, when policy decisions relate to their professions. This oft-noted conflict between bureaucratic authority and professional expertise becomes a focal point of public sector bargaining, and sometimes even overshadows traditional trade union issues involving salary, job security, and other terms and conditions of employment. Bureaucrats will continue trying to constrict and control the members of the library profession. Leaders will empower them to actively participate in the decision making process. Unionization, at least to some extent, forces bureaucrats to give librarians some say in the direction of their own profession.

Another area of note is the sometimes limited and often non-existent right to strike in the public sector. This has led to the development of a complex and highly utilized set of impasse procedures. Mediation, fact-finding, and interest arbitration are more heavily utilized in the public than in the private sector. As the late Dr. George Taylor, father of New York's public sector Taylor Law, stated:

> Labor management relations are an aspect of the broader problem of making democracy work. Ours is a meeting of minds society, and not one that is based on the arbitrary imposition of rules and regulations. A basic concept is reflected in our industrial relations in the proposition that voluntary agreement between the parties of direct interest is the democratic way of establishing the terms and conditions of employment. . . . In our kind of democracy, differences are to be resolved by agreement, or at least acquiescence, in the accommodation which is worked out.

In spite of attitudes such as this, many still feel that the balance of power in the public sector is tipped in favor of the employer. Increased use of impasse procedures are necessary because of this imbalance. Nonetheless, while strikes have a special significance to public employees, the challenge they represent to public policy is a serious one and, thus, the right of public employees to strike shall be strenuously debated for some time to come. In the history of dispute resolution, the right to strike in the private sector remains an important and powerful force. The strike is a legitimate means to be used by workers in pursuing better contract terms. In the public sector, however, the strike is banned in most jurisdictions. Even so, in a few states some categories of public employees have been given the right to strike, subject to certain constraints.

It is argued that the government, representing the public, has the right to expect that its employees will never withdraw their services. Further, the essential nature of government services, and the difficulty of duplicating those services, convinced most policy makers that the strike was an improper weapon in public sector labor relations. As President Calvin Coolidge said, "There is no right to strike against the public safety by anyone, anywhere, anytime."

This point was again driven home with tremendous force when President Ronald Reagan fired all the air traffic controllers during the

PATCO strike of 1980. That had a chilling effect on labor-management relations in both the public and private sectors that is still felt today, as is evidenced by the acrimony shown during the Eastern Airlines machinists' strike of 1989-90, and the Greyhound Bus strike of 1990.

While this hard-line position continues to be dominant in the setting of public policy, contrary arguments are receiving increasing attention. These hold that, except for essential security services, public employees must be allowed to strike if bargaining is to be meaningful. Although this position was largely limited to union advocates, it has recently received some support from public sector management. These officials believe the discipline of the strike will help to achieve more realistic settlements. Most states continue to outlaw the public employee strike. However, a number of states, such as Alaska, Oregon, Pennsylvania, and Hawaii, have made public sector strikes legal, either for most or selected groups of public servants. At least five other states provide for more limited strike rights for their public employees.

There is no constitutionally protected right to strike in either the public or private sector. Any rights that exist, as such, are derived from statute. Sections 7, 8(a)(1), and 13 of the National Labor Relations Act grant and protect the right of private employees to engage in strikes. The framers of that legislation apparently believed that if collective bargaining itself was a social value, then both sides would need to be equipped with weapons strong enough to make the system work fairly and efficiently. Unions were granted the right to strike to counteract the employer's right to the lockout and its other economic weapons. It was also thought that strikes would do the minimum harm to the public good, in that the product market would exercise sufficient discipline on the parties to prevent long and disastrous strikes.

Most states have agreed that the strike weapon ought not to be translated totally into the public sector. It is argued that unlike most private sector employment arrangements, the market exercises very little discipline on public sector employers or employees. Services supplied by libraries and other public agencies are, for the most part, monopolistic. Consumers of these services and employers cannot realistically look to other suppliers, either for the services or the workers.

Another reason state legislatures tend to oppose public sector strikes is their concern that strikes may distort the political process. Opponents argue that elected officials already are under intense political pressure from lobbyists, special interests and political cronies. They ought not to be made to withstand the additional political pressure brought about by a strike.

Proponents of the right to strike argue that it is unfair that a public employee should be denied a right freely granted to a similar employee in the private sector. In New York State, for example, public school teachers may not strike, while teachers in private schools, who are under the National Labor Relations Act, do have the right to strike. The picture is even murkier for public librarians, because of the variety of library financing arrangements which determine the different governing systems of public libraries. In New York State, for example, public librarians in school district libraries or municipal public libraries may not strike, while those employed by association type libraries may strike, even though both types of libraries are primarily supported with tax dollars.

As for the lack of market constraints serving as a deterrent to public sector strikes, proponents respond that the potential for taxpayer revolts has a policing effect similar to that afforded by the market. Similar deterrents can be found in the threats of industries and other commercial enterprises to refuse to locate in communities where public sector employees have shown a propensity to strike.

There are checks and balances on both sides of the issue. The balance of power will be continually changing in response to the dynamics of the labor relations process. Like economics, the laboratory for labor relations is the real world. The doctrine of sovereignty, the lack of available substitute workers, and the monopolistic nature of public services, are not compelling enough reasons to deny librarians, and other public sector workers, the right to strike. This is especially so as the line between public and private sector jobs becomes increasingly blurred, and the notion of essentiality is called into question. Is a striking worker in a plant producing components vital to our nation's national defense, paid for entirely with public money, endangering the public welfare to a lesser degree than a striking public librarian? I think not. The right to strike is a valuable mechanism that is needed in all labor relations disputes, if a fair and proper balance of power is to be maintained. One hopes that future trends will be towards the enactment of more legislation that will give library employees that right.

24. Criticism

*"Maturity begins when we're content to feel
we're right about something, without feeling
the necessity to prove someone else wrong"*
—Sydney Harris

One of the most difficult skills to master for anyone holding a position of leadership is the ability to both receive and give criticism. If you truly are a respected leader, your criticism of the work of your employees will be viewed by them as part of your ongoing training process. If you are practicing MBWA you will be in constant communication with your staff and your contributions as a trainer and a motivator will be done on a daily basis. You also will be in constant touch with the library's customers so that you are able to develop programs and services in response to their needs. In this context, criticism should not be viewed as something to be avoided, but rather as part of the learning process.

A lot of what's involved with being a good leader is much the same as what's involved with being a good parent or a good teacher. It is natural for human beings to want to feel important, to feel that what they think and do matters. If you react to the demands of your public, they will be supportive of your efforts. If you respond to the ideas of your staff, they will feel empowered and will increase their active involvement in the betterment of your library. We can all remember the few great teachers we had that inspired and motivated us. You knew what was expected of you. You were given many tests to prove yourself and you considered the tests to be a fair representation of what you should have been learning. You knew what was expected and if you met the standards the rewards were fair. In other words, the signals given by the teacher were clear. The test review was not a criticism, but rather an integral part of the learning process. Remember how frustrated you were if you were given an unfair test by a teacher who did not adequately cover the material that you were being tested on? You became confused, angry and less motivated.

113

Deal with the problem, not the person. If your criticism is viewed as helpful problem solving, it will be welcomed, not feared. To be effective, communication must work both ways. If the information in your organization is being dispersed from the top down, you have a serious structural defect in your communications system that must be corrected.

Sometimes, no matter how hard you try to involve both the staff and the customers in decisions that affect the library, you will be forced to make decisions that not everyone agrees with. In those instances you may be faced with rather hostile and often abrasive criticism. Hostile criticism from your staff is often an indicator of a deeper, more serious, underlying problem. Either you or your supervisors haven't been communicating effectively, or, as is rarely the case, you may just be faced with a disgruntled problem employee. Identify the problem and correct it. Usually the solution is to provide more training for your subordinate supervisors on how to be good listeners. Listening to employee suggestions, acting on them whenever possible, and vastly outweighing criticism with praise are the keys to high employee morale. Get your people involved and empowered.

It is also easy to discount criticism from an angry customer. Mr. So-and-So always complains about everything, so we just don't pay attention to him anymore. Every library is faced with a few customers who do seem to complain about almost anything. They are the exception, rather than the rule, and even they may have valid complaints that need to be acted upon. No matter how abrasively or annoyingly the criticism is presented, you can't discount the possibility that it may be valid and, therefore, worthy of consideration. Here are a few pointers for handling hostile criticism:

1. Consider the reliability of the source. If the critic has a reputation for making ill founded charges, you naturally wouldn't give the comments as much weight as if they came from a source that you considered to be more thoughtful, but that doesn't mean that you should discount any comments completely.

2. Encourage critics to tell you what they think. Make it clear that you desire their input. Be sincere. People can smell BS a mile away. You will lose your credibility if you have a reputation for mollifying, but not acting on complaints.

3. Understand the criticism completely. Ask for all the necessary information. Go over all the major points to make sure you have the story straight. Absorb everything and carefully consider your response before making a judgment or formulating an opinion.

4. Always maintain control of your emotions. Your presence must be cool and interested. Use appropriate body language to reinforce the fact that you are interested and not angry.

Censorship

Some of the toughest criticisms faced by any library director will be in the area of censorship complaints. I have not included a chapter specifically devoted to this problem, because I see no need to reinvent the wheel. Get a copy of the *Intellectual Freedom Manual*, published by the American Library Association. Read it cover to cover and develop your policies according to its guidance.

Criticism is hard for everyone to take, but it is essential if you are going to run an efficient library that is responding to consumer demand. Criticism must be encouraged and accepted, no matter in what form. You must maintain the image of a thoughtful, patient, and concerned library director, one who is secure enough to place the interests of the staff and the public above your own ego. If you don't have an open mind and the hide of an elephant, you're in the wrong business.

25. Discipline

*"The greatest discovery of my generation
is that a human being can alter his
life by altering his attitude"*
—Henry James

Part of a leader's duties is to apply discipline fairly and uniformly throughout the library. While motivation is the key to employee productivity, discipline is still needed to encourage employees to meet established standards of job performance and to behave sensibly and safely at work. In too many organizations, discipline is counterproductive. The employer is more concerned with controlling employees than in helping them to do good work. Overly restrictive and complex rules and standards will cause supervisors to constantly be met with an array of minor discipline problems. Many discipline problems can be eliminated by the careful screening of potential employees. Ninety percent of the problem is solved by eliminating chronic troublemakers before they are hired. Nonrestrictive work rules, such as flextime, and effective motivation and fair rewards for quality work will eliminate another 9 percent. That leaves the employer with only about 1 percent who cause most of the discipline problems. For most, self-discipline is the best discipline. For those that are either unwilling or unable to practice self-discipline, the supervisor must know how to take timely and effective disciplinary action. This should never be used as a show of power or authority, and should only be invoked when all else fails.

People are less likely to cause discipline problems when the supervisor is a good leader. A leader will show sincere interest in employees, and will create an atmosphere where there is open communication, and one in which the employees enjoy their work, free from petty management tyrannies. If employees find the work uninteresting and the boss unpleasant, it should not be surprising if employees are absent or tardy often, or find other reasons to behave in a manner that will require discipline. If supervisors give employees little chance to show initiative, or to discuss ways that work should be done, employee frustration will result, and this often leads to discipline problems. Personal problems can also lead to employee performance failures, and the supervisor needs to be always alert to that possibility.

When there is an infraction that must be remedied, positive actions such as constructive criticism, instruction and understanding are the best methods of handling it. If it is decided that disciplinary action is warranted, employees expect justice and equal treatment. Being overly lenient with wrongdoers will not be popular with the majority of employees. In fact, such leniency will likely lower morale. The majority of employees who work hard and follow the rules are frustrated and disappointed when they see others get away with improper behavior. To be effective, supervisors must establish discipline through positive leadership. Effective leaders will avoid having to exercise negative discipline through repeated scoldings, suspensions and discharges.

In the event that discipline is necessary, a pattern of progressive discipline must be followed. Disciplinary actions must be applied as equally as possible to all workers. This is difficult to do because of the variety of types and severity of offenses, and the differences in types of personnel and work circumstances. In order for a disciplinary action to stand up in court, or before an arbitrator, it must be progressive in its severity, unless a serious offense is involved. Theft of company property or gross insubordination are examples of serious offenses where progressive discipline would not apply. The library would be justified in firing an employee, for example, who had just assaulted a supervisor for no reason, even if the employee had no other previous infractions on the record.

Here is how progressive discipline could be applied. All of these steps must be taken in a timely manner.

1. Give the employee a verbal warning or reprimand. This step should not be repeated as it is difficult for the supervisor to verify that this was done, and there is a tendency on the part of some supervisors to continue giving verbal reprimands without taking necessary further action.

2. Provide the employee with a written warning, outlining the nature of the infraction and the steps necessary to meet satisfactory standards. Present this document to the employee with a request that it be signed, indicating that he or she has read and understood its contents. If the employee refuses to sign the document, ask another supervisor to be present to witness that the employee has received the necessary instructions and, further, to sign as a witness that the employee refused to sign the document. With each progressive step of discipline, clear explanations should be given as to how the employee can make the necessary corrections, and a definite time limit must be established within which the employee must improve. After the time limit is up, the supervisor must again evaluate the employee to see if the standards have been met. Failure to establish and adhere to a definite time frame in which the employee must improve is a major reason that disciplinary actions are not upheld by arbitrators or the courts.

Depending on the severity of the offense, this written warning may be a letter of reprimand, or may be of a less severe nature, such as a counseling memo. Again, there is the possibility that supervisors will stop at this level of discipline, and repeatedly use the letter of reprimand as a form of punishment. Some bureaucrats take pride in the high number of letters of reprimand that they have issued. Verbal warnings, counseling memos, letters of reprimand, and other forms of discipline will lose their effect if they are repeated with no improvement on the part of the employee, and no further action on the part of the employer. To be effective, discipline must be progressive, uniformly applied.

3. After the first written warning, the second document should be a letter of reprimand. Once a counseling memo has been written, and the offense has not been corrected or has been repeated, the counseling memo should be followed by no less than a formal letter of reprimand. If the violation was serious enough to warrant a letter of reprimand with the first written warning, then this step should be skipped, and you should proceed directly to the fourth level.

Whether to send a counseling memo or a letter of reprimand is a matter of judgment. To maintain consistency, this must constantly be monitored by the director or a high level supervisor. It is that person that sets the tone and maintains fairness and consistency. If that is not done, the system will not work uniformly.

4. Suspension is the next level to be utilized. This could mean suspension from certain privileges, or can mean outright suspension, either with or without pay. This also must be for a specific time limit with improvement expected at the end of it. Again, there is judgment involved here, and constant monitoring is required for consistency. The leader-director will undertake this task willingly and with vigor. The bureaucrat-director will be too busy raising funds, or networking at local, state and national library conferences.

5. Demotion is the next possibility. This cannot be considered for all employees, because many employees are already on the low end of the totem pole. This also should be avoided whenever possible, because it has a humiliating effect on employees and, thus, is usually counter-productive. No time limit need be given. Once an employee is demoted, there is no guarantee that a subsequent promotion will ever take place.

6. Dismissal is the last step and the last choice. All too many supervisors consider this to be a universal cure-all, and they often wish to resort to it immediately, to the exclusion of the other steps. This is not only a good way to destroy worker morale, but dismissal is the disciplinary action most likely to be reversed, unless it is carefully documented and clearly justified. A very lucrative field for attorneys, of late, is the representation of both employees and employers in wrongful discharge suits.

These steps should be followed in any disciplinary proceeding. The yearly or semiannual employee performance evaluation should not be used for this purpose. This document is often misused by supervisors as a disciplinary device. That is one of the reasons that I recommend its discontinuance. Employee performance, if germane to the situation, can be evaluated through testimony. Past written evaluations can be used to cloud the issue, especially if they are old and have been done by different supervisors. Disciplinary proceedings should not be intermingled with employee performance reports. Keep each issue separate. There are a number of considerations that should be used as guidelines in determining the severity of any disciplinary action.

(1) The severity of the offense.

(2) The employee's length of service.

(3) Any provocation that may have led to the offense.

(4) The number of previous offenses.

(5) The nature of any previous offenses.

(6) Previous warnings, or other disciplinary action for previous offenses.

(7) The reasonableness of the library's rules and regulations.

(8) The degree to which the library's rules and regulations have been clearly communicated to the employee.

(9) The consistency of application of library rules and regulations.

(10) Past disciplinary actions for similar offenses by other employers.

(11)   The employee's pattern of conduct.
(12)   The appropriateness of the penalty in relation to the offense.

The "Hot Stove" rule of discipline is often used to illustrate the essentials of a good disciplinary policy.
Advance warning. If the stove is red hot, you ought to be able to see it and know that if you touch it, you will be burned.
Immediacy. If you touch the stove you will get burned right away.
Consistency. Every time you touch the stove you will get burned.
Impartiality. Everyone who touches a hot stove will get burned, because it plays no favorites.

Only a relatively small percentage of any work force ever becomes involved in disciplinary problems. There will always be individuals who find it difficult to accept the regulations and conformity imposed on them by an organized activity, just as there will be individuals who demonstrate occasional minor lapses due to personal or other problems. The great majority of workers usually exert the necessary self-control to keep themselves out of trouble. The state of their morale, however, is significantly influenced by the way in which their supervisors maintain discipline. Leaders make discipline effective by stressing its positive aspects. It should be exercised as much to encourage and reward desirable behavior as to penalize and discourage undesirable behavior. The supervisor's role in maintaining discipline requires unusual objectivity and integrity. The supervisor must not only identify and apprehend transgressors, but also determine the nature of the guilt and impose the penalties. Leaders must possess great wisdom and judgment in the exercise of this authority, or risk reversal of their decisions by higher authority, and loss of respect from their subordinates.

26. Difficult People

"Talk low, talk slow, and don't say too much"
—John Wayne

Difficult people generally regard others as difficult. People who are difficult behave that way because their behavior has produced predictable rewards. They may be only short term rewards, but they are predictable, nonetheless. There are two classes of difficult people that you and your supervisors have to deal with in the public library: the difficult members of the public and the difficult members of the staff. Though these two groups represent two different segments of the population, the methods of dealing with each group are actually quite similar.

People who complain are divided into two groups; one group has a legitimate complaint aimed at improving service or making things work better. The other group are people who gripe about things or give other people a hard time simply because they are acting out neurotic behavior, and through that behavior attempting to exert power over others. Everyone gripes a little bit about a variety of things. That is normal. What is abnormal is the neurotic who gripes about or gives others grief about almost anything. You must be able to recognize and deal with these people or an extraordinary amount of your time and the time of your staff will be spent placating these individuals. If they become too powerful, the will of the majority will be subjugated to the will of the minority of vocal complainers. You must be able to differentiate between legitimate problems for which constructive solutions are offered, and manufactured or imagined problems that are the life's blood of the neurotic.

A neurotic is an individual who consistently acts illogically, irrationally, inappropriately, or childishly. Although theoretically these people are able to think independently, and can generally experience happy living, they constantly fall back on unintelligent behavior, failing

121

to obtain their long range goals and sabotaging their own potentialities. People who work in a public library face much the same problem as police, in dealing with the public; they see not only the worst people, but most people at their worst. Unlike police, however, library employees get to deal, most of the time, with nice people and people who are their best. A trip to the public library is generally a pleasant experience, not anything like the feeling one would experience getting a traffic ticket. The legitimate complainers must be listened to if you are going to run an effective operation. It is only the few who demonstrate aberrant behavior who have to be recognized and dealt with accordingly. Recognizing neurotic behavior takes an innate ability to deal with people and lots of experience. Neurotics aren't easy to recognize. They are great at covering up their neuroses. They don't want anyone, even themselves, to know how illogical they are. When you are dealing with people who are difficult to deal with, you will see an infinite variety of unhealthy behaviors displayed. These behaviors are motivated by indecision, doubt, fear, anxiety, feelings of inadequacy, guilt, supersensitivity, hostility, and resentment. Whether they be members of the staff or the public, these people must be dealt with. You and your supervisors have to develop the mental reflexes to see a punch coming and diffuse its power. Here's some of the punches that may be thrown your way:

1. Critics   The world is full of critics. We even pay some of them to tell us what movies to see, books to read, and restaurants to visit. The critic that is tough to deal with is the one who must offer a negative opinion on everything, whether it is warranted or not. Most critics are frustrated doers who are controlled by fear of failure.

2. Aggressors   These people attempt to get their way with all the grace of an elephant in heat. Aggressors have a burning desire to dominate and control others. They don't know the difference between aggressiveness and assertiveness.

3. Gossips   These people think of themselves as the sole source of information. You usually get a much embellished rumor, instead of real information.

4. Moralists   These people take it upon themselves to tell other people how to live their lives. Moralists see everything as black and white, good or bad and only they know which is which. Moralists like to tell you how to do everything, including living your own life, and are absolutely convinced of their righteousness.

5. Martyrs   These people manipulate others by setting themselves up as sacrificial lambs. Their primary weapon is guilt. The moralist tells you when to feel guilty, while the martyr uses guilt in a covert manner. Martyrs let you know what they have sacrificed for your good, and then are very annoyed when you don't do what they want you to do because of the supposed guilt that you should be experiencing.

6. Steamrollers Don't anybody stand in their way. They interrupt conversations and demand attention in their childlike attempts to control situations.

7. Bombs This is an explosion waiting to go off. Their goal is to frighten you into giving them their way. You must give every matter the same prominence and urgency that these people think it should have. They are very intense and quick to lose their tempers. They are unpredictable, to say the least.

8. Whiners These people find everything wrong and say so repeatedly. Nothing is ever done right. The way things used to be done was always better.

9. Yes people These people agree with everything and everybody. Performance rarely measures up to promises.

10. Braggarts These people always exaggerate their deeds in an effort to make others feel smaller.

There are infinite varieties of these difficult types. Here's some strategies that you can use to deal with them, and keep your own sanity:

1. Develop your skills as an effective communicator. Good communications will help to prevent unnecessary conflicts.

2. Never act defensive.

3. Be assertive, but not aggressive. You don't need to dominate the other party to resolve conflicts.

4. Understand that you have been picked as a target, either randomly, or more likely, because the difficult person fears your talents and abilities.

5. Never retaliate. Don't give these people a hard wall to hit against. Most will be diffused by lack of resistance.

6. Always remain cool, calm and collected. Your body language should indicate clearly that you are in control.

The neurotic behavior of difficult people is something that is part of life. Leaders must not involve themselves in the unhealthy game playing of these people. It takes more than one person to play the game, so why waste your time and energy needlessly by playing. As a leader, you don't have the time to devote to such counterproductive pastimes. Agree politely with difficult members of the public. Avoid becoming embroiled in the games of difficult members of the staff. Your calm handling of the conflicts created by these people will win you the respect of the vast majority of your staff and public who are really quite nice to deal with. Why let a few jerks spoil it for everyone? If you want to succeed as a leader, you and your supervisors must demonstrate great skill in dealing with difficult people. Constant training and positive reinforcement is in order. You should develop sensitive antennae, not horns.

27. Grievances

It is inevitable that some employees will experience dissatisfaction in connection with their work. These dissatisfactions, regardless of whether they are expressed or suppressed, valid or invalid, are referred to as grievances. As the term "grievance" appears in the average labor agreement, it refers to a formal complaint by employees who believe they have been wronged. There is much debate over what actually constitutes a grievance. A good leader will deal with any grievance that the employee perceives to be a grievance. Grievances are best resolved informally through effective supervision and leadership, but they can be resolved through a formal grievance procedure that is usually specified in a labor-management collective bargaining agreement. Unfortunately, many nonunion environments don't provide for the formal handling of grievances. Even if you don't have a unionized staff in your library, it would be wise to institute formal grievance procedures through which employees can have a mechanism that can be used to redress complaints.

Supervisory personnel should be skilled and well trained in handling grievances and should place this high on their priority list if they value high morale and high productivity. Supervisors should act promptly as soon as they sense a complaint or grievance. A gripe, imagined or real, spoken or unspoken, will sap an employee's will to cooperate. Until the grievance and its underlying causes have been examined, the aggrieved employee is not likely to be working up to par.

All grievances must be dealt with in some manner, although not every grievance can be settled to the employee's satisfaction. Some people are just chronic complainers, and it's natural for others to perceive a situation completely differently than the supervisor. When an employee complains about a condition and the facts don't back it up, the best thing the supervisor can do is to demonstrate that the settlement is a just one. Never bluff or try to outsmart an employee, even if that is what the employee is trying to do to you. Grievances are caused by facts, or what the employee believes to be facts. Patience and sincerity are the two most important attributes to employ in settling a grievance. Sometimes just allowing the employee to air a grievance will be enough to settle the matter.

Some of the most common grievances are:

1. Demands for more money.   Employees feel that they are not getting paid what they are worth, or that they are paid less than other people who are doing work that requires the same or less skill.

2. Complaints about job classifications.   Employees feel that a job is worth more than it pays and should be reclassified.

3. Miscellaneous wage complaints.   An employee may feel that there has been a clerical error in calculating overtime pay.

4. Complaints about discipline.   The boss plays favorites. The employee feels that he or she is being penalized for poor work when the real cause was inadequate training.

5. Objections to supervision.   Rules are not clear or clearly posted. There are too many trivial rules and regulations.

6. Seniority.   Seniority may have been calculated incorrectly when the employee was moved to a new position. Layoffs and recalls may have been out of proper sequence. Overtime was not assigned on the basis of seniority.

7. Promotions.   The employee may feel that he or she was not given a fair chance to win a promotion.

8. Disciplinary actions.   The employee feels that the penalty was too severe.

9. Transfers.   An employee feels that he or she has been transferred to an undesirable department.

10. Work assignments.   The employee feels that he or she always gets all the dirty jobs or the worst working schedules.

11. Safety and health.   There is no place provided to safeguard personal belongings. The heat and air conditioning doesn't work. The lighting is poor. Work conditions are overcrowded. Equipment is unsafe.

12. Discrimination.   Men get preference over women. Minorities are not treated fairly.

13. Sexual harassment.   This can range from embarrassing sexual remarks made by supervisors or other employees to denial of pay and promotions for failure to provide sexual favors to supervisors.

Grievances can range from minor problems which the supervisor can remedy on the spot, to major problems that will require the services of an independent arbitrator or redress in the courts. It is hard to pinpoint what situations will lead to grievances, but there are some indicators that an alert supervisor could watch for. First of all, don't lose sight of the fact that grievances are symptoms of something wrong, either with employees, supervisors, or working conditions. Second, employees are most likely to be worried about situations that threaten their security, such as promotions, transfers, work assignments, layoffs, performance evaluations, and streamlining or elimination of their jobs.

The trick lies in detecting situations that breed grievances and then correcting these situations. As a rule of thumb, a good supervisor can reduce the number of grievances by suppressing the "B" Factor, the tendency toward bureaucracy, and applying common sense to relationships with employees. Often supervisors make the situation worse by allowing grievances to fester. The "B" Factor takes effect when a supervisor looks upon a grievance as a challenge to authority rather than an opportunity to correct a wrong.

Supervisors who want to be respected leaders will understand the importance of their role in settling grievances. They should give employees prompt and regular feedback about how well they are doing in their jobs. Uncertainty in this area is a major source of employee dissatisfaction. They should also remove or try to ease minor irritations as they arise. The presence of unnecessary aggravations tends to magnify the more serious complaints when they occur. One of the platform planks of the IWW (International Workers of the World), an early forerunner of the modern labor union, was "freedom from the petty tyrannies of management." This is caused by the tendency on the part of poor supervisors to strive to control rather than lead their subordinates.

Supervisors should listen to and encourage constructive suggestions and, whenever possible, take action rapidly.

Supervisors should be sure to keep their promises. They must know their authority before making a commitment. A nonbureaucratic library director will not only keep these lines of authority clear, but will provide supervisors with as much authority as is necessary to settle grievances at the lowest level possible.

Supervisors should make grievance decisions as soon as possible.

There is nothing worse for employee-management relations than to have management sit on piles of unanswered grievances. If disciplinary action is required, it should remain, as much as possible, between the employee and the supervisor. Always praise loudly and often, but discipline seldom and quietly.

When there is no union involved the following steps could be taken in settling a grievance:

1. Listen to the complaint carefully and attentively. Don't take any grievance lightly. It is important to the grievant.

2. Investigate the facts. Obtain any records or testimony from other employees and the grievant that will clearly establish the facts in the case.

3. Seek expert advice. This won't be necessary for the most simple cases. It would be wise to seek the advice of more experienced supervisors, or to consult the library's attorney, if you feel that a legal issue might be involved.

4. Make a decision based on the facts. Consider each case on its merits. Be as fair and impartial as is humanly possible. Remember that your determination can be overturned by a higher authority. No supervisor wants to look foolish by having an unwise decision overturned.

5. Provide the grievant with a clear, succinct and prompt answer. Explain your position carefully, if it is opposite to the position taken by the grievant.

6. Keep a written record of the entire procedure. Whatever decision you make will set a precedent and you or other supervisors may have to refer to it later in a similar grievance if your library is to maintain fairness and consistency in its handling of employee grievances.

Where a union is involved, the grievance procedure is a very formalized process which is outlined in the union collective bargaining agreement. This will vary from library to library, but whatever the procedure that your library must follow, supervisors should understand it well and stick to it. Although it's still best to settle grievances in an informal manner, experience has shown that where a union is concerned, it is best to be businesslike and stick to the letter of the contract procedure. Sometimes, because of this formality, the parties involved become so engrossed in the process itself that they overlook the real purpose of any grievance procedure—to settle grievances fairly and promptly.

In unionized libraries the labor contract governs day to day employment relationships. The shop steward and the supervisor are the principal interpreters and enforcers of the contract. Differences in interpretation are resolved through the grievance process. This formal process is the mechanism through which employees can voice their disagreements with the way the provisions of the contract are administered. Grievances arise because of (1) differing interpretations of the contract, (2) violations of provisions in the contract, (3) violations of the law, (4) violations of work procedures or other precedents, and (5) perceived unfair treatment of an employee by management.

Grievances may also be caused because employees are generally frustrated in their jobs, or they resent the supervisory style of management, or the union chooses to use the filing of grievances as a harassing tactic against management. Grievances may also be due to unclear contractual language, or may be filed by employees who tend to be chronic complainers or have personal problems. The U.S. Department of Labor has found that the most frequent incidents that lead to the filing of grievances are employee discipline, seniority decisions at promotion or layoff time, work assignments, management rights, and compensation and benefits.

Just as it does in the nonunionized library, effective use of the grievance procedure will prevent small problems from festering and becoming larger ones, and will serve as an effective communication channel between employees and management. In the union environment, grievances serve as a source of data to focus the attention of the two parties on ambiguities in the contract for negotiations at a later date.

The union employee grievance process involves formalized steps for handling an employee complaint. Most union contracts provide mechanisms for the processing of grievances. One is the initiation of a formal grievance—an employee who feels mistreated or believes that some application of policy or action violates rights in the contract, files a grievance with his or her supervisor. It can be done orally, or in writing. The grievant may receive help in formulating and filing the grievance from the shop steward. By far, most of the grievances are settled at this level. The supervisor should not try to blame or find excuses, but rather to solve the problem. A good working relationship between the shop steward and the supervisor will help many problems to be settled at this level.

If the initial parties cannot solve the grievance, it goes to the next level in the hierarchy. At this point the grievance must be presented in writing and both sides must document their case. Contracts may call for unsettled grievances at this level to be filed through several other levels of the hierarchy, before resorting to the next step.

Most union contracts call for a grievance to go to arbitration if the grievance cannot be settled at any of the steps in the authorized procedure. Once the complaint has been turned over to an impartial arbitrator, the arbitrator acts somewhat like a judge, listening to the facts presented by both parties and then making a decision. The arbitrator does not mediate. Both parties agree to abide by the decision. After hearing all the evidence, the arbitrator writes the arbitration award, in language understandable to all the parties involved. The award will serve to clarify the situation to prevent future problems from arising. The arbitrator may review similar cases for precedent, but is not bound by them. More than 75 percent of grievances are settled at the first step, and about 20 percent at the second. Only about 5 percent actually go to arbitration.

Handling formal grievances is a time consuming and expensive problem for all the parties involved. The more grievances that are informally handled at the lowest level possible, the better it is for both employees and management. Whether you are in a union or nonunion library, a formal procedure for settling grievances should be in place and should be strictly followed. Leaders should consistently hone their people skills so as to enhance their ability to recognize problems and nip them in the bud. An indication of effective leadership is often the lack of formal grievances that employees find it necessary to file. Ideally, this is because the supervisor is on the ball when it comes to settling grievances, and not because communication has been stifled.

28. Drug Testing

There's a new dilemma in the workplace: How much privacy must you give up to get and keep a job? Increasingly, employers are probing the personal lives and habits of potential and present employees to determine if they can handle the job. The Supreme Court and also state courts are in the process of deciding several aspects of this matter, one of which is whether employers can use drug testing to screen job applicants. In 1987, according to an American Management Association survey, nearly all of the 995 small to medium size companies surveyed had established a drug testing policy. Federal agencies have far reaching plans in place to perform random drug testing, usually for persons in sensitive positions. Concern for public safety is the main justification for certain occupations, such as air traffic controllers or medical workers. Many question, however, the need to test others whose job performance does not directly affect the safety of others. Library employees would, for the most part, fall into this category.

The nation's leading watchdog of civil liberties, the American Civil Liberties Union, states its fear of the present trends towards compulsory drug testing:

> . . . perhaps the most troublesome aspect of the . . . search question is the readiness with which most people . . . have accepted and indeed, welcomed such procedures. It reflects a disturbing tendency to accept any measures, such as routine searches in public places, which are supposedly devised to protect our safety. Such an atmosphere of acquiescence poses the gravest threat to all of our civil liberties.

The ACLU dismisses all random searches as unconstitutional; others don't. Until drugs are out of the workplace, attempts to test for them will be there too. There are three basic types of testing programs:

random testing, fitness for duty testing, and cause-based testing, each with its advantages and disadvantages. Since one of the disadvantages can include expensive lawsuits, you should learn as much as possible about testing and applicable laws before your library engages in any type of drug testing.

Random testing is performed regardless of whether there is any basis to believe that a particular employee uses drugs. The logic is founded in the program's randomness. Employees will be less likely to use drugs, it is argued, if they don't know when they'll be tested. Fitness for duty testing is aimed at determining whether an employee is capable of performing the job. Such testing is usually part of an overall examination of an employee's fitness, and is primarily used for positions that have significant safety concerns. The most common type of testing program, and the one most likely to pass judicial muster is a cause-based program. Here, an employee is tested only when an employer has "reasonable cause," "reasonable suspicion," or "probable cause" to believe that an employee is using drugs. Employees could be tested, for instance, if they were involved in an accident at work, or exhibited suspicious behavior, such as marked changes in the quality of their work, or changes in temperament, speech, physical condition or social interaction with coworkers.

In the public sector, the choice of programs has been constrained by the limits placed on government by the federal and state constitutions. Various courts have ruled that a drug test constitutes a search and thus may be illegal under the Fourth Amendment, which states that searches by government agents must be preceded by a warrant based on cause. This renders the random drug test generally unavailable to public libraries and other public sector employers.

Library directors must be aware of the myriad legal issues that can arise if their library proceeds improperly with a drug testing policy. Because of the involvement of the state or agencies of the state, public sector employees enjoy greater protection against invasion of privacy than those in the private sector. If a library employee is discharged in connection with a search for illegal drugs, he or she may sue for wrongful discharge, invasion of privacy, slander, libel, or intentional or negligent infliction of emotional distress, to name just a few reasons. The United States Constitution does not expressly provide for the right to privacy. The Supreme Court has recognized that the Bill of Rights serves as a "penumbra of rights" that implies the right to privacy. The right to privacy is implicit in the first, fourth, fifth, ninth, and fourteenth amendments.

Both public and private sector employers may be subject to common law and statutory limitations on substance abuse testing of applicants. Employers and their employees and representatives may be liable for injuries suffered by individuals because of defamatory statements about alleged substance abuse. In some states, false statements may be arguably a basis for a common law claim of intentional or negligent infliction of emotional distress if the statements were made without a reasonable basis for belief of their truth. In unionized organization, the employer-employee relationship is governed by the collective bargaining agreement and by federal laws, including the National Labor Relations Act. In September 1987, the general counsel for the National Labor Relations Board issued a guideline memorandum which stated that under the NLRA, drug testing for both current employees and job applicants is a substantial change in working conditions and thus a mandatory subject of bargaining.

The main reason and justification for drug testing in the workplace is that an employer has an obligation under state and federal statutes to furnish a place of employment that is safe and healthful for all employees, and that is free from employees who are dangerous to themselves and to others. State and federal occupational safety and health statutes and regulations strongly support a public policy for maintaining workplace safety and thus may endorse an employer's drug testing policy. Federal and state legislatures, seeking to clarify the morass of legal and moral issues linked to substance abuse testing, have introduced and enacted legislation or regulations intended to regulate such testing. The courts and arbitrators, in an effort to keep up with the enormous volume of litigation involving substance abuse testing, issue opinions on an almost daily basis.

Many of the state and federal drug testing regulations, already enacted or in the hopper, are being modeled after the Federal Drug Free Workplace Act, which went into effect March 18, 1989. The Act requires all federal contractors and grant recipients awarded contracts or grants of $25,000 or more to certify that they will provide a drug free workplace. The policy applies to all state agencies and departments, many of which rely heavily on federal money to fund a variety of programs and projects.

The Act, which provides minimal guidelines for achieving its goal, has two key provisions. It directs employers to notify their employees that drug abuse will not be tolerated in the workplace, and it requires employers to take action if employees are convicted of violating a criminal drug statute, while on the job. The Act specifically calls for employers to:

1. Publish a policy statement. This statement should follow the guidelines set by the Act.

2. Communicate the policy statement to all employees working on the grant or contract.

3. Establish a drug free awareness program. This program must inform employees of the dangers of drug abuse in the workplace, the company's policy of maintaining a drug free workplace, any available drug counseling, rehabilitation or employee assistance programs, and the penalties that may be imposed upon employees for drug use violations.

4. Notify the contracting agency of any employee's conviction for any drug related violation at the workplace.

5. Impose a sanction on any convicted employee.

6. Make a good faith effort to continue to maintain a drug free workplace. Until regulations are implemented by the federal government, a "good faith effort" means that an employer has instituted a policy and applies it consistently.

While states are taking steps to comply with the requirements outlined in the Drug Free Workplace Act, many do not have comprehensive policies in place. This Act is serving as an impetus for states to adopt their own laws and guidelines regardless of whether they are affected by federal grants or not. As these laws and guidelines proliferate, so too are the court challenges to them proliferating. The battle continues between the need to maintain a drug free workplace and the need to protect the civil rights of the individual.

29. Latchkey Children

"Always fall in with what you're asked to accept.
Fall in with it and turn it your way"
—Robert Frost

Latchkey children have presented a problem for public libraries that they never before had to face to any great degree. Latchkey children are children that have been sent to or left at the public library while the parents or guardians of those children are not present to control their actions. This has always happened at public libraries, but never to such a degree as in the last decade. As more and more women enter the workforce, and the number of single parent families continues to increase, the problem of latchkey children left at the public library is also expected to increase.

In the past, urban libraries found this an annoyance, but were able to cope with the problem. Suburban and rural libraries experienced it to some degree, but hardly enough to notice. Usually the staff took a kindly parental attitude, verbally disciplining the children or asking them to leave the premises if they became unruly. The problem today is much greater, bringing into question such matters as the librarian's role and the liability of the library should a child be molested or kidnapped while at the library. There have even been instances of librarians being called as witnesses in child custody cases involving children left unattended at the library.

Unattended children who use the library for purposes other than materials selection, information, or entertainment, generally fall into two categories. The first category is composed of those children who frequent the library because of its proximity to their school or home. This is the group that simply likes to "hang out" at the library. Librarians have dealt with this group since the doors of the first public library opened. Unless they become unruly or disruptive, their presence is usually not only tolerated, but welcomed. The second group is composed of those children who have been told to go to the library by parents or guardians who have been unable to provide care for them. It is the frequency and length of visits of the latter group that cause the most concern. Children, especially younger children, tend to become bored with little to interest them and in turn become unruly or disruptive. Five year old children found crying in the library because someone has not arrived on time to pick them up after they have been at the public library alone for three or four hours are no longer an uncommon sight. In urban libraries, the sheer numbers of these latchkey children have caused such concern that all the major television networks have presented short documentaries outlining the problem.

Public libraries have a responsibility to maintain order and safety within the library building. This responsibility requires that all public libraries address this problem, and draft and implement a policy for dealing with it. It is a unique problem, because it is not merely an annoyance to library staff and a drain on the library's resources, it is, in many instances, a form of child abuse. These children, for the most part, do not want to be at the library, and certainly not alone, or for such long periods of time. They should not be dealt with as normal discipline problems, because it is the children, themselves, who are the victims. This realization on the part of the staff will help to quell staff frustrations and allow a more positive approach in dealing with this situation.

This problem has been, to some degree, increased by the public's perception, or misperception, of the role of the public library. The library is viewed as a nice, quiet, safe place. Children can spend many hours reading or entertaining themselves with the audiovisual equipment. If there is a problem, the kindly librarian is there to see that everything is all right. The librarian is here viewed in the typical stereotyped role of the gentle spinster whose role is much like that of the children's school teacher. Of course, anyone who has spent more than 15 minutes working in an active public library will know that is not the role or duty of the librarian, and the public library is far from the safest place to leave anyone unattended, much less children. Public libraries are public buildings, and as such, may be entered by anyone—yes, that's anyone: not only normal, well behaved citizens, but criminals, drug addicts, child molesters, mental patients, and any other type of social deviant that is allowed to roam free. The public library may, in some instances, be a less safe place than other public buildings, because the high percentage of female employees may tend to attract potential male sex offenders.

Public libraries are worried about potential liability in this area, especially regarding children who may be injured, molested, or even kidnapped while left at the library. No amount of policy writing or procedural implementation will prevent potential lawsuits. What a carefully thought out and well implemented policy will do is to lessen the chances of successful lawsuits against the library, as well as helping to protect the rights of this new type of abused children.

Keep your policy statement simple. Sometimes people feel that the more they write, the better off and safer they will be. All you are going to do is box yourself into a corner. Follow the K.I.S.S. rule. (Keep It Simple, Stupid!) The policy statement should explain the problem and the policy. The policy statement of the Ames (Iowa) Public Library should serve as a good example:

> The happiness and safety of young children left alone at the Public Library can be a serious concern. Children as young as five have been left at the library for extended periods while parents shop, go to work or, on at least one occasion, drive as far as Des Moines to run an errand. One parent left his three young children at the library for three successive days from 9:00 a.m. till five without providing the children a noon meal. Young children left on their own at the library often become frightened or anxious. Young children may be able to occupy their time for a short while, but, being children, soon become bored and restless, disturbing the enjoyment of others.
>
> The following policy and procedures seek to address these concerns for the children in a responsible manner. It is not the Library's intention to seek out unattended children but rather to have a reasoned response prepared as problems present themselves.

This addresses the problem clearly, but could be considered a little too wordy and unnecessarily outlines some real cases, possibly opening up the library to a libel suit. A better example is from the Pioneer Multi-County Library System in Oklahoma:

> The Pioneer Multi-County Library System staff hopes that the children who use our libraries will perceive our facilities as warm, inviting and fun places to be. Many programs are offered to make libraries enticing to children and to help children enjoy their visits and develop a love of books, reading and libraries!
>
> But, when children are left unattended for several hours when no library programs are being offered, they often become bored and disruptive.
>
> Each year in the United States, over 50,000 children are abducted and never found. Young children are not safe when left unattended in the

library. The staff cannot know if the children are leaving the building with parents or with strangers. For the protection and well-being of children who enjoy our libraries, the following policy has been established.

The part about the abducted children may be a little alarmist, but maybe not. Both these libraries have taken a positive stand without emphasizing negatives, such as statements that indicate that the library is not a free baby sitting service or a day care center. The second part of the policy statement should be a statement of the policy itself. This should be brief and to the point, such as:

Parents may not leave children under age ten unattended at the library. Parents are responsible for their children's behavior while at the library. Disruptive children ten or older will be asked to leave after receiving one warning. [Flagstaff, Arizona]

(Why the age restriction? What happens to disruptive children that are under age 10?)
Far better is:

The Dallas Public Library welcomes children to use its facilities and services. However, responsibility for children using the library rests with the parent/ guardian or assigned chaperon, not with Library personnel.

Here is an example of a policy statement used by the Middle Country Public Library in Centereach, N.Y., that is not too long, over explanatory, or alarmist. This is a conglomeration of many sample policies and was formulated in close consultation with staff professionals dealing with children:

The safety and well being of young children left unattended at the library is of serious concern. Young preschool children left on their own often become frightened or anxious. Older school-age children may be able to occupy their time for a short while, but, being children, soon become bored and disruptive, disturbing other patrons and requiring unreasonable attention and supervision on the part of the library staff.
The following policy seeks to address these concerns for the children. It is not the library's intention to seek out unattended children, but rather to have a reasoned response prepared as problems arise. The policy states:
Parents, not the library staff, are responsible for the behavior of children using the library. Parents will be notified if their children are left unattended and require supervision. If parents are unavailable, proper authorities will be contacted.

Do some research. Ask other libraries to send you their policies. Then come up with a concise policy that will address the needs of your library. Some advocate, besides policy statements, lengthy definitions of the problem, such as defining what are unattended children, vulnerable children, or what is disruptive behavior. If you start down that path, you're going to end up with a cumbersome procedural manual that has about as much use as your other cumbersome procedural manuals. Over reliance on such documents will tend to limit your flexibility, and will place you in a position that does not allow movement to deal with future unexpected problems. You're going to spend most of your time revising the manual instead of dealing with the problem. An important part of the follow-up to a policy statement, however, is the proper training of staff.

The policy that you develop should be developed with input from the staff that is in direct contact with the public. Don't develop a policy first and then inform those that must implement it afterwards. That is not only insulting and demeaning to your staff, it's just bad leadership. Matters, such as when to call parents, or the police or child welfare agencies, must be developed with careful consideration of staff experience. There are no hard and fast, cut and dried rules. These are decisions which require the judgment of experienced professionals. There must be constant training and vigilance in this area, as well as consistent supervision by top management, to make sure that this policy is being administered uniformly.

Remember, we're not cops, social workers, or teachers, even though we get to do all of those jobs at one time or another. This is a problem that is not going to go away any time soon. The quicker you face it, and develop policies to deal with it, the better off your library and all the children who use your library will be.

30. Circulate: Don't Store

"I take a simple view of life: keep
your eyes open and get on with it"
—Laurence Olivier

Because of the lack of clearly defined goals for many public libraries, they are operated more like academic libraries than public libraries. As Charlie Robinson, the director of the Baltimore County Library in Towson, Maryland, said in a September 1, 1989, *Library Journal* article, "Can We Save the Public's Library":

> [S]ince the founding of ALA in 1876, public librarians really never have faced the challenge of clearly defining the role of the public library as it differs from that of the academic library. That's not a problem for academic or school libraries. They know exactly what they are about. Public libraries don't, as evidenced by our pathetic attempts to be all things to all people—pathetic because our limited financial resources assure us of failure in any one area of service as a result of trying to be successful in all.
>
> ... being "all things to all people" has characterized the historically perceived responsibilities of public libraries as institutions designed "to save and share" books. Pretty clear, pretty basic, and, in my view, pretty wrong. Saving books for future needs, needs which cannot in any way be clearly seen and clearly delineated, is the responsibility of academic libraries and, obviously, the Library of Congress, insofar as it serves as the national library.
>
> Saving books is absolute poison to effective public library service. Yet many of us, trustees, librarians, and members of the public, see that warehouse function as a primary function of public libraries.
>
> ... [P]ractically no one has ever given any thought to differentiating between collection development for public libraries and that for academic libraries. That is collection development relating to materials which the public wants, rather than those which librarians divine as "the best reading."

If you think Charlie doesn't know what he's talking about, check his circulation figures. They're astoundingly high. Whether he realizes

140

it or not, Charlie knows one heck of a lot about marketing and economics.

This attitude towards collection development is intellectual elitism masquerading as professional public librarianship. It is not the function of the public librarian to decide what should be stored for future reference, or what are the "best" materials for the collection. It is the function of the public librarian to provide library services that will be most cost effective and useful to the largest segment of the public. Instead, many librarians devote the lion's share of their library's resources to serving a relatively small portion of the population, who are supposed to receive service from libraries designed specifically to service their needs, namely school and college libraries. Too many public librarians love to buy books that no one will use, while they hate to buy books that will be heavily used.

The answer often given to this criticism of elitist librarians is, "If we just bought what the public wanted, we would have nothing but junk in the library." First of all, so what! And second of all, who gave these librarians the job of being the cultural arbiters for their community? I know a library director who will only buy videos that meet the library's "high" collection standards, while his public is clamoring for the latest popular movies. So he continues to buy operas and cooking demonstrations that collect dust on the shelves, while refusing to buy popular videos that his public would actually use. It's almost as if he thinks there is something wrong with people using the materials in the public library. It's all right to buy both if your library has the money, but if it doesn't, and most libraries aren't that wealthy, the popular materials should be given first preference. This reminds me of the librarians I was forced to endure as a child. There would be hell to pay if the book you read got a fingerprint on it. Books weren't things to be used and enjoyed, but only revered and saved, fingerprint free of course.

Academic book selection is basically divided into two categories; first you buy anything that the professors ask you to buy, and then with any funds that are left, you buy items which the collection development people have determined should remain in the archives because they may be of some future research use. School libraries, when they have money, which isn't often, buy books that supplement the school curriculum. In both cases, purchasing decisions are based on the perceived needs of their constituents. Public libraries, on the other hand, often try to guide their constituents along a more enlightened path. Those that have little contact with the public purchase materials that they feel will enhance the library's collections. Materials that duplicate those already in the collections of college and school libraries are also purchased without a second thought. The same librarians that will do that, will resist buying 100 copies of a best seller even if demand warrants it. Research materials will sit on the shelves for months or years, hardly touched, while people often have to wait months for their names to reach the top of the reserve list for a best seller. If Sears was run like that, they'd be out of business.

Just the mention of Sears or the supermarket approach to public library service should be enough to bristle the hair on the back of the neck of one of our intellectually elite brethren. "We're not a supermarket. We're an educational institution," they'll scream. The public library is, in fact, an educational institution and because of that it tends to attract the same kinds of educational bureaucrats that populate our nation's schools. Academic freedom has allowed them to determine what is culturally and intellectually proper for the rest of the world. Although I don't necessarily believe that is even a good attitude for education professionals, I won't argue the point here. The point here is that these people have no place in the public library. They should stay in the educational community and leave public library service to those who have a respect for the public that they serve. Mr. and Mrs. John Q. Public, however plebeian librarians may perceive them, are the people who pay the bills. They should get what they pay for. Public library collection development should be based entirely on consumer demand, not on the tastes of librarians.

Besides failing to buy titles that people want in sufficient quantities, many libraries devote an unnecessary amount of their resources towards protecting what the library has purchased. This is especially true today with the introduction of new materials into library collections such as computer programs, compact discs, and especially, videos. Librarians will go to extraordinary lengths to restrict and protect those materials. Every library engages in some reasonable, cost-effective, protection procedures such as a restricted entrance and exit or an electronic theft detection system. What has happened recently is that public librarians, in their theft paranoia, have instituted procedures that are so labor intensive in nature that their cost far outweighs the alternative costs of actually having the materials stolen.

I occasionally am called on as a speaker or consultant concerning library video collections. I always recommend that videos, like all library materials, be kept on open shelves, and attractively displayed as in video stores. (Video stores want people to rent their videos.) I also recommend that any library that is initially starting a video collection be prepared to budget much more than they anticipated, because video will shortly become their library's highest circulating collection. When the collection is initially being developed and funds are limited, buy all the popular materials first and the more esoteric materials later. For most, their budgets will never allow them to purchase esoteric materials.

Occasionally, there is a glimmer of light. Yes, we really do have some great public librarians. There's just too few of them. These folks are eager to learn and are thrilled to be able to introduce a new service that will be heavily utilized. The all too common reaction, however, is one of disbelief and skepticism. There is often a committee that has been formed of librarians and trustees to discuss the merits and standards of a video collection should their library start one. This has delayed and perverted the process of getting the customer and the product together as efficiently and as soon as possible. Libraries that have instituted video collections frequently refuse to buy sufficient quantities of popular materials, usually claiming that their budgets won't allow it. Budgets should be based on consumer demand. We shouldn't dampen consumer demand by failing to provide the proper amount of products and services. What would happen to a department store if it failed to provide its customers with the products and services that they wanted?

Videos are an excellent example of what's wrong with many of our public libraries. Never before has a service offered by public libraries taken off so rapidly and met with such widespread public support. If a library in one community has a good video collection, then the taxpayers in the neighboring communities notice and pressure their libraries to do the same. A library's poor collection development and poor marketing skills usually merely show up as anemic circulation. In the case of video, it has manifested itself in vocal and persistent citizen complaints, thus forcing many elitist libraries to offer the service, even though to do so is most repugnant to them. They often subtly resist by providing only a small collection of extremely boring materials, and claim that budget constraints prevent them from doing more. Videos should be placed on open shelves. Most people never talk to a librarian, or use the card catalog. The majority of library materials circulate because people browse through the collection. Restricted video collections not only prevent browsing, but also will greatly increase your library's labor costs. Librarians seem to have a pronounced blind spot in this area. One library I consulted with informed me that the theft of videos was so great that they were placing the videos on closed shelves. Patrons would have to search a card catalog, and then would present requests to a staff member, whose job it was to retrieve the videos from the forbidden area. When I explained to the librarian in charge that labor costs of this procedure were in excess of $50,000 per year, she was stunned with disbelief. I was as stunned when she informed me that the entire loss to the library in the past two years from lost or stolen videos amounted to only $5,000. The replacement cost to the library was actually much less than that figure because many of the videos lost did not have to be replaced and the videos that did need to be replaced could be purchased at prices far below their original purchase prices. The idea of spending $50,000 in labor to prevent a $5,000 loss doesn't make much sense to anyone, except, I guess, an elitist librarian. You don't have to be an economist to understand the implications of that cost-benefit analysis.

Libraries that market their services, and design those services to meet consumer demand, will have the highest circulation figures and the highest satisfaction ratings from their customers. Your job is to bring the customer and the product together as rapidly and efficiently as possible. If your library is doing that, it's because you've got what they want and you help them to find it! Think about that the next time you frequent a department store in which you enjoy shopping. The public library should not be a museum or an archives. It should be the department store of libraries. Plebeian, maybe, but wonderful, nonetheless.

31. Library Building Design

*"Simplicity carried to an
extreme becomes elegance"*
—Jon Franklin

Closely akin to a library's ability to provide services that are
responsive to consumer demand is a library's ability to provide a pleasant, safe and efficient workplace as well as a pleasant, safe and efficient
place for its customers to "shop." To quote the venerable Charlie
Robinson again:

> The academic library building and most of the equipment in it is totally
> and absolutely inappropriate to a public library. Yet in many cases public
> libraries continue to replicate these buildings for general public use. I often
> run into architects who cite their experience with a library building—
> almost always it is an architect who has been infected by conversation with
> an academic librarian instead of a shopping center architect.
>
> What about equipment? Libraries are full of shelving and 98 percent
> of the public libraries have almost totally steel bracket shelving, which was
> designed for storage, not merchandising. Perfectly appropriate for savers,
> which academic libraries are. Perfectly ridiculous for public libraries,
> whose responsibility is to get materials out of the building for people who
> are alive now, not to store them for future generations.

The public areas of public library buildings should follow closely
the design of the modern department store.

1. It should be comprised of great, flexible, wide open spaces. The
only constant is change itself. The library building must be easily adaptable to change. People should not have to adapt themselves to the
building. The building should be adapted to meet the needs of the people. Take a good look around the next time you're in your favorite
department store. Displays and departments are always changing to
meet the changing tastes of the public. The store is of a large open
design, so that its interior fittings can be easily changed.

2. It should have little or no windows. Windows are for aesthetic

145

value only. They reduce the amount of wall space that can be used to display library materials. No one can read in the library by sunlight. Even libraries with lots of windows have to leave the lights on all the time anyway. Were you shocked or horrified at your last trip to the department store that there were no windows? You probably never noticed, because you were too busy looking at the racks of merchandise that were displayed to attract your attention. The lack of windows will also reduce vandalism, because there will be none to break. This will in turn help to reduce the library's maintenance and insurance costs.

   3. Display as many materials as possible on open faced shelving, much like that used by bookstores.

   4. Provide convenient parking as close to the building as possible. Stay away from decorative islands, trees and other forms of beautification in the parking lot that your architect will insist upon, especially if you live in a cold part of the country. These things may be pretty, but they make snow removal a nightmare in the winter. Even in warm climates such objects are an undue hazard for motorists, who are constantly backing into trees or running over the concrete islands that are especially hard to see at night.

   5. Use solid, old fashioned, block and brick construction. Your architect will probably come up with lots of new ideas to experiment with. Modern techniques and materials are great to use in finishing the building, but in any case, be very wary of anything that isn't tried, tested and true, when it comes to basic construction. The basic structure of the building should be of sturdy stuff. Under no circumstances accept less as a supposed cost saving. I have seen one library building which had an exterior facing of brick. This brick was separated by thin steel studs, from the inside wall, which was only a thin piece of plaster board. There were no cement blocks used at all. There was lots of glass, which lessened the shelving space and increased the vandalism problem, as well as contributing to the general lack of stability of the building. It looked fine, but it wasn't. This is a multimillion dollar library building that could have a hole broken through its wall by one good swift kick. The swift kick would be better delivered to the architect and the library director.

   Form follows function. There is nothing wrong with creating a beautiful library. It's just that function too often takes a back seat to form, and the library staff and public have to spend the next thirty years paying for the problem.

   6. When designing your building make sure that the architect

knows that you are the boss. You want a building that will be operationally efficient, have low maintenance costs, and will be of lasting value to the community. You don't want a building that wins an architectural award for the architect, but that is a horror to operate.

7. Involve all levels of your staff at all times in the planning and construction stages. They'll know many things that the bosses won't, and input from them is absolutely essential, if your building is to be efficient and responsive to staff and public needs. Again, this is another way of empowering those in your library who are in contact with the customers.

8. Design staff areas with sufficient room for your people to work. This involves understanding what they actually do, or might be doing in the future. Most public library work areas are designed with too little office space because the director doesn't understand what the staff really does, or could be doing. I have seen many public libraries with virtually no office space for the professional staff, because the director thought that their only function was to answer reference questions in the public area. Work areas, like public areas, should be large, open, flexible areas, that can be easily changed. Check out any modern office building. The work and office areas are all created out of movable walls and furniture which can be easily adapted to changing needs. Don't lock your people into your concept of what they are presently doing. Even if you're right, the work situation will change by the time the building is completed and will continue to change as long as it is in operation. The work areas, like the public areas, must be large and flexible enough to accommodate both present and unanticipated future needs. Don't force the staff to adapt themselves to the building. Create a building that can be easily adapted to changing needs.

9. As opposed to the public areas, don't skimp on windows in the staff areas. The work areas should maintain an atmosphere of openness and freedom. Provide staff with the best furniture and equipment that you can afford. It is the cheapest in the long run. It's the people who are your largest expense. Providing them with the proper facilities and tools with which to do their work will increase efficiency and lower operating costs. Morale will also be raised because you have shown them that you care enough about them to provide them with these things. If you like to sit in a comfortable chair, so does your staff.

10. Provide as many restrooms in as many areas of the building as possible. Public restrooms should all have changing tables for parents with babies. At least some of the staff lavatories should have

showers. If you have a wellness program, this will give your staff a place to shower after exercising and would also be much appreciated by maintenance staff, by allowing them to clean up after a messy job.

11. Provide space in every work area for the staff to wash their hands, make coffee and have a snack. This will increase efficiency, because it lessens the need for staff members to adjourn to the water cooler or staff lounge to do something as simple as getting a drink of water, or a snack. Refrigerators and microwave ovens in all work areas are a must. Employees who are allowed to have coffee or cola at their desks while working will be happy employees, and will appreciate the fact that you have given special consideration to their needs.

12. Offices of the director and other supervisory personnel should not be near the public areas, surrounded by glass, so that they can oversee the activities of the public and staff. You are not the captain of a ship, and even the captain of a ship has a private office where private business can be conducted. Offices are used to conduct work in quiet and privacy. They are not to be used as observation decks. If you want to find out what's going on with your staff and your public, go to those areas of the building where they are and get busy practicing management by wandering around.

13. Assign someone from the library staff to act as the library's agent in supervising the construction of the building. This job does not require any technical knowledge. If technical questions need to be answered, that's the architect's job. This staff member is there to see that the library gets what it's paying for. You don't have to be an engineer to know if the correct light fixtures or door knobs are the ones that are being installed. This person should work closely with the architect. The knowledge that this person will acquire during the construction phase will greatly enhance the library's bargaining position in any disputes that may arise among the contractors. If they know that you are there and have a good idea about what's going on, you are much less likely to get a snow job, if, for example, one contractor tries to blame shoddy work or lack of progress on the shoddy work or lack of progress of another contractor. This job must be filled by a high level employee who anticipates a long term relationship with the library. That is the incentive to make sure that things are done the way the library wants them done. This person will have to live with any problems after the architects and contractors are gone. Because they will have a vested interest in the long term use of the building, they will more clearly understand that what might appear to be short term cost savings on construction may well turn out to be long term operating expenses.

This is not supposed to be a cram course on how to design and build a library building. It only outlines some of the basic principles that, if followed, should increase your chances of producing a building that is not only beautiful, but efficient to operate. Remember, it is you and your staff who are going to have to live with this building long after the architect and contractors have left. It's your library, not the architect's. You and your staff must take an active part in its design and construction. Get what you want, not what somebody else thinks you need. Don't let the "B"-for-Bureaucrat Factor take over by becoming overly reliant on the credentials of "experts." The long run costs of building an efficient library will be small in comparison to the continued savings in staffing and other long term operating costs.

32. Automation

"The only way of discovering the limits of
the possible is to venture a little way
past them into the impossible"
—Arthur C. Clarke

The library is a business. Like any business it can experience productivity increases through automation. Automation is especially important in public libraries because one of the library's most important functions involves the storage and retrieval of information. The basic function of a computer is to store and retrieve information. Although the benefit of computerizing many labor intensive library functions is patently obvious, public libraries have lagged far behind other businesses, and even other public agencies, in incorporating computers into their operations.

Not only are public libraries slow to utilize computers, the computer operations that have been given the most emphasis are the same as those emphasized for college libraries; complicated database networks designed to support interlibrary loan. Except in the smallest public libraries, circulation control has been catching on, and that is one bright sign that some of our colleagues have at least begun to understand the concept of productivity. The main emphasis in introducing automation to public libraries should be in the areas where the greatest productivity increases will affect the greatest number of people: acquisitions, collection development, personnel work, and other matters of general administration. Those are exactly the areas where automation has been least utilized.

Only a small percentage of people using the public library use the card catalog at all. Most people browse or will ask the staff for help in doing unsophisticated research. Well trained professional staff should be available in sufficient numbers to perform that function. Yet in spite of this, millions and millions of state and federal dollars are each year poured into library automation to support sophisticated networked databases. The vast majority of public library users could not care less whether materials in the databases have full MARC entries, much less even knowing what that means. An equally small number of public library users ever use interlibrary interloan (ILL) at all, and the great majority of those users are school and college students who are supposed to be served by libraries specifically designed to meet their needs.

The cheapest and most efficient way to provide public library service is to have a well designed building of sufficient size, stocked with a collection that is large enough to satisfy the needs of the library's customers. Obtaining books by ILL is a very expensive, labor intensive procedure. It serves only the smallest percentage of library users, yet it receives the lion's share of automation funding. New York State has even gone so far as to spend millions of dollars on school library networks. Can you imagine? Millions of state tax dollars spent on databases to send Dr. Seuss from one library to another. Any kid can tell you what's wrong with school libraries: they are not open convenient hours, they often provide no reference service because they aren't staffed adequately, and they don't have enough books. School library networks have been sold, as have other networks, as a great cost saving through the sharing of resources. But ILL is actually the most expensive way to provide library service imaginable. It's just that the real costs of ILL are usually hidden at the local level through subsidies that are provided by a higher level of government. In New York State, millions of dollars are wasted annually on useless and outdated library systems, while public libraries receive almost no state funding that could be better used for such purposes as improving library staffing, library construction, or other such mundane matters as actually buying library materials that the public could use. The higher the level of government, the greater will be the influence of the "B" Factor.

So where and how should automation be used in the public library?

1. Circulation control. This is where a lot of the action is, so it will fit the bill of allowing the greatest number of people to benefit from productivity increases. Use a computer system from a company that will design one to fit your needs. If you don't think that there is a computer service out there right now to fit your needs, keep looking. One is sure to turn up soon. The current revolution in automation is like nothing ever before seen in the history of mankind, so it requires that you refocus your thinking or you will be left in the dust. Bureaucrats who are relying on committee studies to develop the "perfect state of the art system" will never get one. Even people who resist innovation and change sometimes realize that change does occur, however slowly. In the case of computers, changes are happening at a rate never before experienced with any other technological innovation. Computers are becoming smaller, more powerful and cheaper at an astoundingly rapid rate. Library bureaucrats who are waiting for the perfect system will never get one because the "state of the art" will be changed by the time the one chosen is installed. Pick one, get going, and be prepared to upgrade as technology changes. In the computer business, the time frame for long run decisions is about three months. For the short run, check your watch.

Don't network your circulation computer system with any other libraries. The ILL advocates will be aghast at this. "Why have a computer if you can't do interlibrary loans with it?" they will say. One library that I studied is recently in the process of converting to a free standing system and pulling its resources out of a database network with about thirty other libraries. This library circulates about one million books per year. Out of that, only 3,000 ILL were circulated. When all the costs were calculated, such as staff costs, computer costs, and telephone line charges, the costs of obtaining each of those 3,000 books via ILL was so high that using the money to buy the books and simply giving them to the other libraries would have been a reasonable, cost saving alternative. The cheapest thing in the long run would have been for the other libraries to have bought the books themselves. That would have saved staff costs on both ends of the ILL chain. Bureaucratic librarians don't like to do cost-benefit analyses, especially when it comes to ILL, the perennial pet project of our professional elite.

2. Collection database.   If you're going to get a computerized circulation system, you might as well combine it with the automation of your card catalog. You can't use a computerized circulation system anyway unless you have converted most of the information from your card catalog. Too many libraries have ended up wasting unnecessary time and spending more money than they should have because these two functions weren't combined. Once this is done, then you will be ready for a totally integrated computer system that will not only handle all your business procedures, but will service your needs in the areas of acquisitions and collection development. The instant a book is ordered for a customer, that fact will be available to all, at any computer terminal in the library. No more thumbing through reams of paper order files. Weeding, and other matters concerning collection development, will be greatly improved because of the computer's ability to accurately record what materials are actually being used. Weeding will no longer be educated guesswork. Your computer will help your staff to judge much more accurately what should be thrown out and what should be added.

Don't get talked into any interim technology, such as compact discs, for this purpose. Unless you have an extremely small collection, there's just too much information for compact discs to be both efficient and cost effective in this area. There are lengthy time delays in updating compact discs and, over the long run, the costs are enormous compared to computers. This is because every update involves reproducing the compact discs with all your bibliographic information on them, not just what has been added. Each user station also needs its own compact disc, because most compact disc systems don't allow internal networking. With a computer system, you have instant access to every bit of information as soon as it is fed into the system.

It has often been said that most of the public hardly ever uses the card catalog and those that do, don't know how to use it correctly. That won't be true of a computerized card catalog. The next generation knows how to use computers and enjoys using them. This phenomena is going to increase at geometric rates. The computer will be as common in every home in ten years as the television set is today. The library's card catalog will be no further away from the library's customers than the nearest home telephone modem.

3. Internal office and personnel procedures. If you want to figure out what portions of your internal office procedures can be computerized, just look at anything that is being accomplished involving paper; punching time cards, filing papers, or typing any variety of things on various forms of paper. If you are still using a lot of paper procedures, then your library is probably operating at a productivity level that has not been improved upon since the turn of the century. Before the computer, the typewriter and the telephone were the only two major technological innovations that provided significant productivity increases for office work. If you're not using computers, you are basically doing things the way they were done 75 years ago. Anything that presently involves paper can be accomplished more efficiently and stored more rapidly using much less space when it is computerized. There is no library today that is too small or too poor not to afford a computer. If you don't have one, it is costing you many times in personnel costs what the computer would cost. Here are some office procedures that should be converted to computer operations:

a. Acquisitions. There no longer need be a cumbersome central paper file, which is difficult to check. Every computer terminal in the library would have immediate access to library acquisitions.

b. Time keeping. There are several very sophisticated time keeping systems on the market right now that eliminate the need for time cards and provide supervisory staff with a wealth of information that they would have never believed possible. One library even uses its computerized staff time cards as coded keys to permit access to the staff areas, thus greatly enhancing security at no cost whatsoever. There are even systems out there that will prepare the entire payroll for you, including printing your checks. The biggest plus in this area is that all payroll records, which usually must be saved indefinitely, can now be stored on computer diskettes, thus greatly reducing the need for storage space.

c. Payroll and personnel record keeping. Again these procedures can be speeded up at astounding rates, while at the same time reducing the amount of personnel required to perform them. You will realize significantly higher and more efficient output, use far fewer input resources, and require little storage room: That's productivity.

Your staff will think up lots of new ideas for using your computers to increase productivity. Many libraries are lagging behind in their conversion to automated technology, especially in the areas of general library administration, because of the "B" Factor. The boss thinks that he or she has to come up with all the ideas about how computers can best serve the library's needs. Often a system is chosen and a terminal is plopped down in front of a staff member, who is then told to use it. Instead of happy and creative cooperation, the boss is more likely to meet with resistance, because the staff member hasn't been involved in the process—i.e., hasn't been empowered.

I have seen many library directors who proudly extol the merits of automation. They have installed automated catalogs and circulation systems first, because that was what the majority thinking of the profession told them to do. They did this with little or no consultation with the members of their staffs who are in direct contact with the public, or who are actually doing the work in the business offices. Some of them even have computers on their desks and they love using them for writing memos, board minutes or some other mundane purposes. The staff are the last ones to be consulted about the computer, as well as being the last ones to get to use it. This is backwards. It is exactly the opposite way that it should be done. Instead of the staff's being empowered to innovate, they have been stifled. Here's a better way, a way that works wonders:

Advise the staff on some things in the library that you feel might be adaptable to computer technology. Then leave them alone. Let them discuss the matter and decide on what system best suits their needs. Stand back and watch, but offer only minimal guidance. Obviously, you don't want them to order a $1 million computer system, if you could get along with one for only $10,000. If you give them some general financial guidelines and explain that whatever system they order must be adaptable and expandable to meet future needs, needs that may involve things that no one has thought of yet, you will be pleasantly surprised. All artisans know that their work will be greatly improved if they have the best tools to work with. Your staff will know the same thing. They want to do the best job possible, and if you provide them with the best tools to do the job, they'll use them to everyone's best advantage. Yes, even in ways that the bosses never envisioned. Get the ideas to generate from the bottom up, not the top down.

If you asked someone to start a business, then provided an unsafe and undersized building in which to work, and insufficient staff given old fashioned tools with which to do their jobs, would you be surprised if that person couldn't compete in the marketplace and produced a shoddy product causing ultimate failure of the business? Of course not! Yet we see this every day in the library business. Unfortunately, poorly run monopolies rarely are forced to go out of business.

33. Marketing Quality Services

"What kills a skunk is the
publicity it gives itself"
—Abraham Lincoln

The public library is like no other public institution. It must market its services much like a private business if it is to attract customers. If a private business attracts customers, its revenues usually increase and it is able to increase production to meet increased consumer demand. Libraries run on yearly budgets, which must predict consumer demand far in advance of receipt of the funds necessary to provide desired services. This causes a dilemma for the public library, especially with some of the public libraries' newly introduced services, like video, which have expanded at a rate never before experienced.

This chapter is not about how to do publicity and public relations. Most libraries do an amazingly good job at that already. From making use of print ads, and television and radio, to producing their own advertising brochures, libraries are leaders in the public service business, in their abilities to get the message of what they offer out to their constituents. What this chapter is about is the attitude or the marketing strategy, if you will, that should be employed when offering and advertising those services.

Businesses attract customers for a variety of reasons, such as price, service, location, variety, and quality, to name just a few. Customers do not usually stay with a company when the products it offers are sold on the basis of price alone. What good is a low price, if the quality and service are poor? There are some people who like to shop only at cheap discount stores, and will buy only on the basis of price. Most others, however, take into account many other factors when choosing where to spend their money.

Businesses also cannot stay in business in the long run when they only sell on the basis of price and do not make enough of a profit that will allow them to invest capital in future development. Profits are needed for research and development. Products must be constantly improved, and the efficiency with which they are manufactured must also be constantly improved. If a company does not maintain and improve upon its plant and equipment, it will eventually fail to maintain its competitive status. Libraries should not sell their services on the basis of price alone. Other factors, especially quality, should be stressed as part of the library's marketing strategy.

Our colleagues in the public education community have fallen into the trap of trying to please everyone and then marketing their product on the basis of price only. Look where it's gotten them. They used to be respected institutions. Now they are viewed as big, bloated bureaucracies and are constantly under attack for their inability to produce a quality product. People are no different when it comes to paying their taxes than when they buy something at a department store. They are willing to pay a little extra for quality and service. This can be seen in community after community as public usage figures represent the quality of the library's services and the library's ability to market them effectively, rather than the size of the population served.

People who live in wealthy communities have always known this. One of the main reasons that they have high and stable property values is because they provide quality local services. The value of homes and the success of local consumer businesses in any community are in direct proportion to the quality of that community's parks, schools, fire service and its public libraries. These people take pride in their community and are willing to spend money on their public services because they realize that such expenditures are a good long term investment in their communities.

We sometimes miss the point when selling library services to poorer communities. This, again, is due to the elitism demonstrated by certain members of the library profession. The library elite not only think that they know what is best for the communities they are serving, they think they should market their services, for the most part, based on price. This is selling most people short, as is the case with most elitist attitudes. All people, not just rich people, want to feel pride in their community. If you sell your library based on quality, you will still get people complaining about their taxes. These people will complain no matter what their taxes are. The majority of people actually have no idea how much they pay in library taxes, or any other taxes, for that matter. What you need to tap is the wellspring of support that can be found in the members of your community who want to feel a sense of pride and ownership in their library.

Your library will be worth more if you have added higher value (quality) to its services. People are willing to pay more when they realize that there is higher quality in the services that they are buying. Always strive for quality, not just low price. When the staff and the members of the public develop a feeling of ownership and pride in their public library, the support you will receive, from both the producers and the recipients of your product, will be greater than you ever imagined. You won't need to spend so much money on publicity and public relations. Word of mouth will sell your library. Pride produces quality, and quality sells itself!

34. Meetings, Memos, Manuals

*"Most of our so-called reasoning consists
of finding arguments for going on
believing what we already do"*
—James Harvey Robinson

Although the matters addressed in the title of this chapter have been covered in other areas of this book, they are of sufficient importance as to merit separate and distinct mention. Meetings, memos and manuals are among the favorite trappings of the bureaucrat. It is through these devices that bureaucrats enhance and enlarge their empires and impede the work of others. These are the things that make life worth living for any bureaucrat. These are tools that are used by management, and like any tools they must be used judiciously and with skill. Misuse of these tools will hinder, not help the productive process.

Meetings

Formal meetings should only be called when absolutely necessary. Absolutely necessary, in this context, means a grave crisis where it is necessary to get your people together as soon as possible to impart vital information that cannot wait for a later time. Management consultant Peter Drucker, in *Management: Tasks, Responsibilities, Practices*, says, "The ideal is the organization which can operate without meetings. . . . The human dynamics of meetings are so complex as to make them very poor tools for getting work done."

Never schedule regular staff meetings that are held at a certain date and time each week. These are the type of meetings that bureaucrats love, where various staff members are asked to report on their department's activities, and are critiqued on same.

These meetings formalize what should be informal. If you become skilled at practicing MBWA you will find that the need for such meetings is gradually reduced to the point that it will become obvious to everyone that they are not needed. Such formal meetings serve to stifle communication rather than to enhance it. The most productive form of communication is informal, private, one on one.

Consider, also, the costs of holding regularly scheduled meetings. Multiply the salaries of the people at the meeting by the time spent at the meeting. More often than not, you will find that you have spent $1,000 to solve a $100 problem. Keeping the cost-benefit analysis of meetings always in mind should help you to constantly evaluate your need to call them.

Call formal meetings only as a last resort. Before calling any meeting, always ask yourself if that is the ideal way for you to be communicating with your staff. Most often, the answer will be a resounding "No!"

Memos

Never write a memo unless it is of the CYA (cover your ass) type. This is the type of memo that you publish to show proof that you have complied with some legal requirement, such as overtime hours, promotion procedures, or rules concerning health and safety. This type of memo is written as much to legally protect the library as to inform the staff of its contents. Use them sparingly.

Whenever you write a memo, remember that the written word will be interpreted differently by different people. Always explain to your supervisors the reason for the memo and explain its ramifications thoroughly. Follow up to see that your supervisors personally convey your explanations to everyone on their staffs. Personally sample the comments of staff members at various levels to make sure that the information and attitude that you want conveyed to your staff has been communicated to them in the way you intended.

Never write a memo to the general staff to outline a problem that affects only a few. Everyone will be looking around to see if you are blaming the problem on them, instead of the staff members who committed the offense. Memos outlining problems, in general, tend to emphasize in the minds of employees that they have been written to blame and chastise, rather than to learn through mistakes.

Try using departmental newsletters to impart information to your staff in place of memos. This is a much lighter, friendlier way to keep people informed about what's going on. If the writer has some talent, and personal information about birthdays, engagements, etc., is included, newsletters can be quite a bit of fun and can serve as a significant morale booster.

Avoid writing memos whenever possible. Memos tend to come across to staff members as overly serious, or scolding in nature, if they outline a problem that has occurred. If the memo was meant to correct a problem, the best and most effective way of communicating information is through personal contact (MBWA). Never substitute a memo for personal contact, and never write any memo that has not been followed up with personal contact.

Manuals

Manuals are the rulebooks that are the scar tissue of past mistakes. They are created by people who wish to avoid those mistakes in the future. The problem is that no one ever reads them unless there is a mistake, and then they only use the manual as a source to assign blame.

Take all your procedural manuals and throw them away. You should have some basic general guiding principles to which your staff adheres. Your staff should understand the tone you have set, the ethics and standards involved, and the ultimate goals of your library. You have set the course. Let them figure out how to get there. If your organization is truly committed to change, it will be changing so rapidly that you will not have the time to be constantly revising detailed procedural manuals. The manual will be always out of date.

Meetings, memos and manuals, if improperly used or overused, will make your library's administrative functioning too rigid, too analytical and too formal—all things that are revered by bureaucrats but that should be abhorred by leaders. Use them sparingly and judiciously.

35. Recruitment and Training

"Talent is as talent does"
—Malcolm Muggeridge

The recruitment of the brightest and the best into the library profession will be, for the foreseeable future, hindered by the long lasting stereotypical image of the librarian and the work that he or she supposedly does. People basically enter any field of work for a variety of reasons, the most important of which are:

1. Prestige. Surveys have repeatedly shown that the library profession ranks the lowest on the prestige scale, lower even than teaching. People may be attracted to such professions as medicine and the law for reasons of prestige, but you'll never meet anyone who entered the library profession for that reason.

2. Money. Strike two! Nobody ever entered the library profession to get rich.

3. Working conditions. School librarians may be attracted because of the short hours and short school year, but certainly not public librarians. Today's public librarians are faced with a variety of overlapping shifts, juggled into a seven day workweek. In many libraries they are not adequately compensated for shift work or for overtime, Sundays, holidays and other premium time work. The library profession too often tolerates working conditions that weren't acceptable to automobile workers in Detroit in the 1930s. Almost strike three, but not quite.

4. Interest in the work itself. Here the profession is again hampered by the stereotypical image of librarians and the work that librarians supposedly perform. These present difficulties in recruiting new professionals. When people do decide to enter the profession, too often it is for the wrong reasons. They think they are entering a profession that will give them a nice quiet place to hide from the public. Public service in a modern public library requires a type of person quite different from those the profession too often attracts.

162

In spite of this, public library service attracts a surprisingly large amount of devoted advocates. Once prospective librarians understand what public library service is really about, the outgoing types who enjoy providing service to the public are attracted and for the right reasons. Unfortunately, the first three factors still weigh heavily against us, and thus we are experiencing a marked shortage in talented public librarians. Even though there is a shortage of librarians, the incentives for people to enter the profession are still so sorely lacking that library schools across the country continue to close for lack of students.

How can this be remedied? Easy! Increase the prestige, increase the remuneration and greatly improve the working conditions. There isn't much that can be done about the profession's prestige in the short run. The prestige of the library profession will increase, in the long run, when the money greatly increases and the working conditions greatly improve. This will be the result not of a plethora of committee studies on the changing needs of the library profession, but rather on economics. As the demand grows greater and the supply gets smaller, pay and working conditions must improve in order to attract more people of high quality into the field.

One thing the library profession needs to do is get rid of the apologetic wimps and self-sacrificing hypocrites who blithely accept inadequate pay and working conditions. We need to reward those who have fought to improve their lot. They have not only served to improve conditions for themselves at their own libraries, but have also served to raise the standards for all. In the long run, that is the only way that the library profession is going to meet its needs both in the areas of quantity and quality.

I know of one public library that has simply given up trying to recruit prospective candidates from the local library schools. There have not been sufficient numbers of candidates interested in public library work and those that were interested were of such inferior quality that it would have entailed greatly lowering the standards of this library to have employed them. Instead, the staff actively recruits candidates from the community at large. They have encouraged talented clerks and pages, who were attending college while working part-time at this library, to go on to library school. These people decided to enter the profession because this library had set a standard for excellence that served to attract quality personnel. This library has also found a rich source of candidates in former teachers, who had left teaching years before to raise their families and were eager to return to the work force. Out of pure necessity this library had discarded traditional recruitment methods, and instead had realized that the work force available to them at present was far different from the one from which they had recruited in the past. In this way, they have not only been able to recruit a sufficient number of librarians, but have developed a staff of personnel truly dedicated to public library service. These were people who knew what the public library was about and entered the field because they enjoyed the work. They strive to be the best, and they are treated as such with pay and working conditions that set the standard for the rest of the profession. Improvements in pay and working conditions have always been tied to productivity increases. This library has enriched its staff by not enlarging its bureaucracy. Even though it pays the highest salaries in the industry, only 50 percent of its budget is comprised of salaries, an amazingly low figure by any standard.

You can't change the world overnight. Pay attention to your library and do the best you can to improve salary and working conditions there. You will not only be helping your library, but the library profession in general.

Once you have these people, make sure that you spend sufficient time and effort training them. Library school has taught them some of the technical aspects of their jobs. This is not nearly enough if they are going to be successful public librarians. You must truly believe that 98 percent of your people are terrific, and you must constantly train and encourage them to become passionate and persistent advocates of innovative quality public library service.

Here are some simple training tips:

1. Encourage all your staff, professional and non-professional, to visit as many other libraries as possible. Even the worst libraries have some good ideas that you will be able to use.

2. Send staff to management training seminars and bring in outside trainers to hone staff skills in leadership. There are many companies out there that will do this for a reasonable fee. Your staff will not only enjoy this training, but will also realize that you care enough about them to want them to be the very best at what they do. Respect for the worth and dignity of every individual in the library is a must if morale is to remain high.

3. Avoid sending staff to the usual library committee meetings that produce nothing but reports. Attendance at state and national conferences has some value, but its main attraction still seems to be a free vacation and an invaluable network for job hunters. Consider how

many libraries spend a fortune sending the director and trustees to these meetings, when they won't spend a dime on staff training? Nauseating, but true!

4. Provide time and expenses for staff to take advanced studies in related fields, such as business administration, computer science or labor relations. Public schools have encouraged such advanced study for years. What's the matter with the library profession?

5. Always train your people to handle the next level of supervisory authority. One of the main functions of a leader is to train other leaders. Library directors too often don't provide adequate staff training and development because they practice top down, instead of bottom up management. They think that the staff doesn't need to know anything more than the basic mechanics of their jobs, because only the director or a few other high level mucky-mucks can have any good ideas. Too often, directors are locked into inactivity because of a concept that is known as "learned ignorance." The real world is not neat or predictable. There are a lot of variables which constantly serve to mess up our rational analysis. Ignorance is usually equated with lack of knowledge. However, ignorance itself may be desired, by some, when retaining such ignorance suits personal purposes. Many directors are willing to exert great efforts to preserve their ignorance, in order to avoid turmoil and the stress involved with change. Learned ignorance occurs when there is a rejection of useful and valid information for primarily self-serving reasons. The status quo is safe and secure, so it is encouraged at the expense of experimentation and change.

No public library director can afford the false comforts of intentional ignorance. They must be alert to its symptoms and fight them always. Break the rules. Encourage growth and change. Get the best for your people, and you'll in turn be more likely to keep getting the best people. Once you've got them, encourage them in every way possible. The best of the best, if encouraged and nurtured, will beat the others by a mile, and will set a new higher standard which the others will strive to achieve. That's better for your library and better for our profession.

36. Institutional Culture

"Together we will build a team that will create and maintain an atmosphere of mutual trust and respect, listen to the people who do the work, hold team members accountable for results, with team members given great flexibility in deciding how to achieve results, with the clear understanding that ethical standards must never be compromised"
—H. Ross Perot

Each library has a culture all its own. In the business world, this is sometimes referred to as corporate culture. In the public sector, it's institutional culture. Institutional culture is a flavor, a feeling, an atmosphere that pervades the institution. It is impossible to see, and difficult to define, but it is there nonetheless, and it will be reflected in the attitudes and behavior of the people who work at your library. If you have developed a bureaucratic culture, then employees will behave like bureaucrats and will be rewarded like bureaucrats. If you have built a culture where leaders are rewarded for productivity, creativity and innovation, then your people will be affected by that attitude and will alter their behavior accordingly. Attitudes determine behavior and behavior affects courses of action that will be taken, for good or bad.

This is an area that is given much lip service by phony leaders. These are the people who have read all the newest management books and can quote, at will, management's latest gurus, but through their actions they serve to create an institutional culture that is exactly the opposite of the one they profess to believe in. Leaders strive to create this culture, not through the statements they make, but through the actions they take and the examples they set. It's the boss who sets the style for the organization. You may be able to fool yourself and your superiors, but you'll never be able to fool your subordinates. Your actions will develop the culture, and that, in turn, will have a great effect on your library, especially in the areas of planning and problem solving.

Planning is important if your library is going to keep up with the times and meet the future needs of its customers. Planning is totally worthless, if you haven't clearly identified the long range goals of your library. Only after you have a good idea where you should be headed can you plan on how to get there. Here's a few pointers on how to plan effectively:

1. Every library should have a long range plan. Never forget that form is not more important than substance. A plan must be realistic and flexible enough to be implemented. All too often, I have seen planning become an end in itself, rather than a means of achieving a goal. Library directors have spent many wasted hours sitting on planning committees whose only function was to produce a written plan that was placed on a shelf to collect dust, while a new planning committee was being formed to start the whole process over again. Planning should be brief, basic, and should project ten to twenty years into the future.

2. Plans should be constantly reviewed and updated to meet changing needs and incorporate technological advances. This is one of the reasons that you must keep plans simple and stick to basics. There is a tendency to get locked into a predetermined plan even though a change in data or a technological advance has made it necessary to alter the plan. This is one of the reasons that libraries have lagged behind in the use of automation and the introduction of nontraditional library services, such as video. Alter the plan to meet changing needs, don't alter your thinking to fit the plan.

3. Promote from within. One of a leader's most important functions is to train other leaders. Too many library directors spend their time in bureaucracies training loyal followers. Good followers do not make good leaders. That is the reason that so many libraries look to the outside to fill high level positions. If your employees have not been trained to move up the ladder, you are sending them a very clear message: you do not respect or trust them. They are not worthy of higher office.

There are major libraries out there, with literally hundreds of employees, who don't have one single person on the staff who is capable of moving to the director's spot. Those libraries are perpetuating an institutional culture that says, "Stay with us a while, build your resume, and then move on to a higher position, somewhere else." Why should anyone who works in a library like that be concerned with the library's long range goals? Only low level employees will be there for any protracted period of time. High level employees only move up the ladder by building a resume which is based on short term accomplishments.

I know of a library director who feels that library directors should be hired by a federal agency, and that they should move from job to job, every two or three years, so they can find out what's wrong and shake things up. This guy was describing the job of an auditor, not a library director. Unfortunately, our profession continues to reward this type of short term job hopper.

4. Never create a title for a job before it exists. People, especially those with a tendency to become bureaucrats, are very impressed with titles. If you make up a fancy title, with a restrictive job description, you'll go a long way towards helping a potential leader become a fledgling bureaucrat. They will become impressed with the importance of the title and will tend to limit themselves to only those duties in the job description. Allow people to set their own goals and design their own jobs. They will be much more productive. After they have done so, give them a title that fits what they are doing.

5. Throw all of your procedural manuals in the garbage. This is another area where form becomes more important than substance. If your library is changing and developing at a rapid pace, your staff will spend an unnecessary amount of time revising procedural manuals that are hardly looked at anyway. The workforce is changing and the nature of work is changing. Recognize and accept that, and your focus will always be on productivity, not image. Going by the rule book may be safe and secure, but it is certain to stifle innovation and creativity.

6. Always be aware that innovation, creativity and other unforeseen events will alter the plan. One of the reasons that the roads on Long Island are so overcrowded is that when planners projected twenty years ahead to judge how many cars would be on the road, they projected their figures based on how many cars each household had at the time the plan was developed. They based their planning on population increases only. The flaw in the plan was that time and circumstances altered the amount of cars owned per household. Although the population was projected with some accuracy, the plan was way off because the number of cars owned per household had risen at a greater rate than the population. The plan should have been altered to account for a change in one of its factors. It wasn't, and the result is crowded roads and more costly catch-up road work.

Don't get locked into any plan just for the sake of following the plan. We still are getting very expensive and little-used networks forced down our throats, because the bureaucrat planners of the past decreed it to be so. Rigid plans, like bureaucracies, can take on a life of their own, and will be extolled long after they have become outdated and useless, by armies of faceless bureaucrats who refuse to be deterred by anything so simple as common sense.

7. When planning, always keep in mind the Five P's: Proper Planning Prevents Poor Performance.

How the people in your library go about solving problems is, to a large degree, influenced by the culture that you, as a leader, have created in your library. Encourage the following thoughts to rise to the top, and keep the "B" Factor from influencing your staff's problem solving:

Failure should not be fatal. Thomas Edison once said that he failed his way to success. People learn from mistakes.

Solve a problem only if there is one. "If it ain't broken, don't fix it." There are quite enough problems to handle without having to reinvent the wheel.

Encourage the use of common sense in solving problems. Don't use committees for this purpose for any reason. You'll get a watered down committee report, designed to please everyone and offend no one. That's no way to solve a problem.

Use the service of supposed "experts," such as lawyers, accountants and architects, only when absolutely necessary. There are times when experts are needed, but, all too often, people check their brains at the door and turn everything over to an "expert" when it comes to dealing with problems. That's how we get library buildings that are designed by architects who have no understanding about how a public library really functions, and sets of financial records that only make sense to the accountant who made them so complicated.

I once had a librarian who worked for me who was wonderful at dealing with her subordinates. When it came to problem solving, and decision making, however, she fell short. She felt unsure of herself and constantly referred problems to higher authority or the "experts," when she should have solved them herself. Our computerized circulation system went down one day, and her immediate reaction was to call in "experts," in this case the computer company and an electrician. She was later embarrassed when the electrician had identified the trouble with the computer. Someone had knocked the plug out of the wall.

Delegate responsibility and authority. Responsibility for details teaches employees to function independently, and giving them the authority to get things done allows problems to be solved at the lowest level possible. Encourage solutions to generate from the bottom up, not the top down.

When solving problems, always explain why, or ask the reason why, when someone else is describing the solution to you. When I was a young army lieutenant, I was given the responsibility of taking a convoy of twenty vehicles to our new post, a distance of some four hundred miles. The officer who instructed me before departing handed me a gasoline credit card and told me to fill up the trucks right before I got to the Thruway. As I approached the Thruway, I noticed that the gas tank on my vehicle was still reading nearly full. I decided to push on and fill up the vehicles later, someplace on the Thruway. The vehicles began to run out of gas before we were halfway through our journey. It was then that I realized why I was told to fill up before I got on the Thruway. There were no stations on that road that would accept the credit card that I was given. My commander should have explained the reason for his orders and I should have asked why.

Make decision makers out of your people. A staff that has been trained not to think or make decisions is not productive. The monkey-see, monkey-do mentality that creates employees who function as assembly line drones went out with the thirties. In today's organizational environment, people must be able to think and act as independently as possible.

There is a lot of talk today about making the job fun for your people. Happy workers are productive workers. Working in a bureaucracy isn't fun, even to the bureaucrats. These are usually very serious folk, indeed. If you want your people to have fun, which, in turn, will increase productivity, strive to create an institutional culture that makes them feel part of a team. Encourage everyone's active participation and involvement in the planning and decision-making processes of your administration and constantly reinforce that feeling by acts that show that such participation is desired and respected. Do that and your library family will not only have fun, but will make you look good by providing your public with a great library.

37. Success Summary

*"The successful people are the ones
who can think up things for the
rest of the world to keep busy at"*
—Don Marquis

There is often a great disparity between what supervisors think is necessary to motivate employees to do their best and what employees really need to do their best. This has never been more clearly demonstrated than in the well-known survey of the ten things that supervisors thought employees wanted from their jobs, and the ten things that employees actually wanted from their jobs.

Here is what the supervisors who were surveyed thought their employees wanted, in order of preference:

1. High wages.
2. Job security.
3. Promotion in the company.
4. Good working conditions.
5. Interesting work.
6. Personal loyalty of supervisor.
7. Tactful discipline.
8. Full appreciation of work done.
9. Help on personal problems.
10. Feeling of being in on things.

Here's what the employees surveyed actually wanted:

1. Full appreciation of work done.
2. Feeling of being in on things.
3. Help on personal problems.
4. Job security.
5. High wages.
6. Interesting work.
7. Promotion in the company.

8. Personal loyalty of supervisor.
9. Good working conditions.
10. Tactful discipline.

All human behavior has a purpose, meets a need, and has a payoff. Human beings don't generally engage in random behavior. They behave in a manner that is designed to help them achieve predictable goals. Bureaucrats serve to pervert human behavior towards short term, low productivity goals. Form becomes more important than substance. Leaders understand the magic of positive motivation and use it to best advantage. Here's a summary of strategies that you can use to increase your effectiveness as a leader:

1. Behavior is goal-oriented. People do things for a reason. Understand the reasons and you can modify the behavior.

2. Achievement is always tied to feedback.

3. People are more innovative and productive when they are allowed to set their own goals and standards.

4. Communicate to employees that you are eager for them to succeed in their jobs in a way that is personally rewarding to them.

5. People tend to behave as others expect them to behave. Expect the best from people and you will usually get it.

6. Make people feel that they are part of a team, or better yet, a family.

7. Encourage regular, open and informal communication. Keep your people informed of any new developments, no matter how minor, and encourage them to offer suggestions. Utilize their suggestions as much as possible.

8. Promote from within. One of the functions of a leader is to train other leaders.

9. Stress quality, enabling people to feel pride in the services that they are offering.

10. Reduce distinctions of rank between levels of management. Bureaucrats are more concerned with perks than productivity.

11. Create as pleasant a workplace environment as possible.

12. Don't lay off staff without trying to place them in other jobs within the library. This is especially applicable when automation warrants staff reductions. If displaced employees can be absorbed into other jobs, they are more likely to encourage, rather than resist, automation.

13. Be a good listener. When you talk, you only repeat what you already know. When you listen, you learn.

14. Delegate, especially authority and responsibilities for details, so that people may learn to function independently.

15. Always give credit where credit is due. Never take the credit yourself for your employee's efforts.

16. In most circumstances, never give an order. Make a request and explain the reason for it.

17. Be consistent, both in personal temperament and, as far as is humanly possible, in treating everyone the same.

18. Always emphasize the positive, play down the negative.

19. Actively seek the counsel and help of all your employees.

20. Use every opportunity to build up the self-esteem of each employee.

21. Always let your people know where they stand.

22. Choose your words carefully. Employees will remember an intemperate remark long after you have forgotten it.

23. Give employees every opportunity to take part in decisions, particularly those affecting them.

24. When you are wrong or make a mistake, admit it.

25. Develop a healthy sense of humor. Laugh the loudest if the joke is on you.

26. Use common sense when problem solving. Maintain a skeptical view of the opinions of "experts."

27. Plan carefully and thoroughly, but don't get locked rigidly into any plans. Innovation and creativity are more important than sticking to a predetermined plan.

28. Never forget that substance is more important than form.

29. Identify and focus on general goals and steer towards them. Strive to be a visionary.

30. Never forget that it is the boss who sets the style for the entire organization.

31. The keys to any leader's success are trust and respect. You can demonstrate trust through your actions, but you can never force people to give you respect. Respect must be earned, and it can only be given voluntarily.

Keep this list in a handy place and refer to it often. It will be helpful in what should be any leader's life-long battle with the "B" Factor.

Index